To Light a Thousand Lamps

A Sunrise Library Book

To Light a Thousand Lamps

A Theosophic Vision

Grace F. Knoche

THEOSOPHICAL UNIVERSITY PRESS
PASADENA, CALIFORNIA

Theosophical University Press
Post Office Box C
Pasadena, California 91109-7107
www.theosociety.org
2001

Copyright © 2001 by Theosophical University Press

All rights including the right of reproduction in whole or in part in any form, except by a reviewer who may quote brief passages to be printed in a newspaper or magazine, are reserved under International and Pan-American Copyright Conventions.

∞

The paper in this book meets the standards for permanence and durability of the Council on Library Resources.

Library of Congress Cataloging-in-Publication Data

Knoche, Grace F.
  To light a thousand lamps: a theosophic vision / Grace F. Knoche
    p. cm.
  Includes bibliographical references and index.
    ISBN 1-55700-170-7 (cloth : alk. paper)
    ISBN 1-55700-171-5 (pbk. : alk. paper)
  1. Theosophy   I. Title.
BP570.K565 2001
299'.934—dc21   2001006910

Printed at Theosophical University Press
Pasadena, California

Contents

	Foreword	vii
1	What Is Theosophy?	3
2	Evolution	13
3	The Quickening of Mind	23
4	Reincarnation	31
5	Death: A Doorway to Light	41
6	Remembering and Forgetting Past Lives	49
7	Karma	59
8	Karma and/or Grace	75
9	The Christian Message	83
10	Western Occultism	101
11	Psychism	113
12	The Two Paths	129
13	The Pāramitās	137
14	H. P. Blavatsky and The Theosophical Society	145
15	Who Will Save Us?	157
16	The Daily Initiation	171
17	A New Continent of Thought	183
	Sources	193
	Index	199

Following in the footprints of sages of a hundred past generations, I sow the beautiful seed for thousands of years to come.
— I-TSING, 7th-century
Chinese Buddhist Scholar

Foreword

LEGENDARY AND WRITTEN TRADITION testify to the presence throughout time of a brotherhood of men and women scattered over the face of the globe who resonate with the spiritualizing impulses reaching earth from higher regions. Their recognition of one another is not dependent on outer insignia but on inner communion. Such was the case with I-tsing, translator into Chinese of hundreds of Buddhist Sanskrit texts, and his assistant, Chēng-ku. When they met it was as though they had known each other "from former days," and after becoming conversant with the largeness of their mission Chēng-ku said to I-tsing:

> When Virtue wishes to meet Virtue, they unite themselves without any medium, and when the time is about ripe, no one can stay it even if they wanted.
>
> Shall I then sincerely *propose* to propagate our Tripiṭaka* together with you, and to help you in lighting a thousand lamps?†

When virtue meets virtue — how better describe the experience of intuitive recognition? Perhaps this may explain, in part at least, the global awakening now taking

---

*The "Three Baskets" or major divisions of the Pāli Canon.

†*A Record of The Buddhist Religion as Practised in India and The Malay Archipelago* (A.D. *671–695),* I-tsing, p. xxxvi.

place, where thousands of men and women of varying interests and backgrounds, knowingly or unknowingly, are on the same wavelength: they are fired with the urgency to do all in their power to help turn humanity from senseless self-destruction to thoughtful self-regeneration. They labor for the safeguarding of human dignity and self-worth, for the protection of our planet, and for the building of a new type of civilization founded on the brotherhood of all life and the joyous collaboration of peoples and races for the benefit of the whole of humanity.

At the same time, this is a period of great uncertainty, when all that human beings most value is being weighed in the balance. Will we individually and collectively have the insight and courage to make the transformation from egocentricity to a perspective of planetary and solar dimension? In fact, this is already happening in the quiet, like the seed germinating under the snows of winter. So, rather than concentrate on the ugly and poisonous in human relationships, let us celebrate the joy of life. From the wonder of birth to the still beauty of death — both phases of *life* — all is transformation, change, flux, ebb, and reflux. The outbreathing of divinity brings worlds, humans, atoms, and suns out of the Unknown into visibility, enabling each to express a little more of its potential. The cycle completed, the inbreathing, inrolling, or withdrawal of the life energy follows, the shedding of forms releasing consciousness once again into realms vastly ethereal.

There is never a poison but nature has an antidote. Just as scientific ingenuity has provided us with the means of race suicide, so current efforts to synthesize Western scientific intuitions with Eastern mystical thought are furnishing us with tools for our emancipation — *if* we have the heart and the will to utilize them for beneficent ends. Take, for instance, the concept that the physical universe is analogous to a hologram, where the three-dimensional image may be projected from any portion of the negative: this is extremely suggestive, especially if applied to the human being as a spiritual intelligence. Moreover, it is a striking parallel to the wisdom-teaching once held worldwide that every life-spark comprehends the whole.

By various metaphors an ancient Buddhist sūtra brings the point home that every being and thing partakes of buddha-essence. In one example, it envisions the Primal Buddha (Ādi-Buddha) on a thousand-petaled throne, each petal a universe which comprises a hundred million worlds, each of which in turn has its own suns and moons and minor buddhas of the stature of Gautama, who himself is "a minute portion" of the original essence of Buddha. So likewise every particle of dust contains "Buddhas without number."*

Small wonder that people through the ages have venerated gods as races of beings whose obligations toward their earth children — immature gods — impelled them to remain among the young humanities until they were off to a sound start. Their protection will never cease: karmic links of compassion and responsibility were forged in long-ago world cycles of evolution. We too are bound by unbreakable ties with the kingdoms younger than our own, and in

---

*Avataṃsaka-sūtra (Flower Garland Sūtra, *Kegon-sūtra* in Japan). Cf. *Japanese Buddhism* by Sir Charles Eliot, pp. 108–10.

like manner by karmic necessity in future cycles will aid them by stimulus and love.

Pursuing the thought further, we intuit something of what the sacrifice of a Gautama or a Jesus means to us today. The Christian dogma of Vicarious Atonement hides a profound esoteric fact: the divine concern that prompts a bodhisattva or christos to imbody on earth is, in very truth, a continuing benediction. This means that humanity is now, as it ever was, the beneficiary of the ongoing altruistic labor, not only of enlightened ones who periodically imbody among us, but also of the acts of love of unnumbered people who, consciously or unconsciously, inspire others to light their own lamp of compassion.

In every age and among every people are born those to whom matters of the mind and spirit are of paramount importance. Almost from birth they seem guided by an inner compass to search out the hidden, causal springs of human existence and learn how they might effectively help ease the burden of human sorrow. Perhaps they are revivifying a quest anciently begun in former lives. Certainly there is a mystic knowledge that speaks to the soul, a boon granted those who qualify by lives of dedication to truth and to humanity's need. Known by many names in different eras, this god-wisdom has been handed down through the millennia as a sacred trust by generations of sages who through initiatory experience have verified the facts of Being. Pivotal in the current awakening was Helena Petrovna Blavatsky who inspired all who were receptive to "sow the beautiful seed" of theosophic wisdom far and wide for succeeding generations.

At the onset of a new century and a new millennium, this study is offered in profound gratitude to HPB and what her sacrifice and magnificent philosophy have meant to the world and to the writer.
— G. F. K.

The Theosophical Society
International Headquarters
Pasadena, California, USA
July 11, 2001

Acknowledgments

Every book represents the efforts of many people, and I wish to express my gratitude to each and every member of the editorial and printing staff. More particularly, I thank Eloise Hart for bringing together the initial material, much of it originally having appeared in *Sunrise* magazine, Sarah Belle Dougherty for her editorial assistance and for the index, Jean B. Crabbendam for checking the index, Elsa-Brita Titchenell for invaluable help in the revision process, Jim and Ina Belderis for checking the quotations, Randell Grubb for his assistance throughout and for assembling the references, and Will Thackara for his valued critique and for supervising the book's production. — G. F. K.

To Light a Thousand Lamps

What Is Theosophy?

THERE IS A WISDOM-TRADITION THAT once was universally known by every people on the face of the globe, a common treasury of inspiration and truth from which the saviors and benefactors of mankind draw. Known variously in different eras as the perennial philosophy, the *gnosis* of Greek and early Christian thought, the esoteric tradition, or the Mystery-teachings of the sanctuary — it is this god-wisdom that Jesus shared with the fisherfolk of Galilee; that Gautama imparted to ferryman and prince; and that Plato immortalized in letters and dialogues, in fable and myth. Today the modern presentation of this wisdom is called theosophy.

What is theosophy? The word is of Greek origin, from *theos*, "god," and *sophia*, "wisdom," meaning "wisdom concerning divine matters." As a term it has a venerable history, having been used by Neoplatonic and Christian writers from the 3rd to the 6th century AD, as well as by Qabbalists and Gnostics in an attempt to describe how the One becomes the many, how divinity or God manifests itself in a series of emanations throughout all the kingdoms of nature. It was in use during medieval and renaissance times, Jakob

Boehme being called the Teutonic Theosopher on account of his vision of man as microtheos and microcosmos.

The word *theosophia* has also been linked to Ammonius Saccas of Alexandria who, in the 3rd century AD, is said to have imparted to his pupils a theosophical system or school of thought in an attempt to fuse into a universal synthesis the seemingly divergent elements of the archaic wisdom then current in that teeming metropolis. Of exemplary character, he was called *theodidaktos*, "god-taught," on account of the divine inspirations he received. Ammonius exacted the strictest morality and although no record of his teachings or practices was made, providentially his pupil Plotinus later recorded for posterity the salient teachings of his master. Thus we have the *Enneads* or "Nine" books of Neoplatonism, which have exerted a profound influence through succeeding centuries.

Later in Europe, Qabbalists, Alchemists, the early Rosicrucians and Freemasons, Fire Philosophers, Theosophers, and others pursued the self-same purpose. Singly, and in secret associations, they held that the One, Divinity, the indefinable Principle, emanated forth from itself the entire universe, and that all beings and things within it will ultimately return to that source. More specifically, they sought to inject into the Christianity of their day the signal truth that mystical union with Divinity was *everyone's* birthright because within each human being is a divine kernel.

Clearly, then, the theosophic endeavor, its teaching and practice, is not a new movement. It is ageless, rooted in the infinity of the past as firmly as it will be rooted in the infinity of aeons to come.

What is this theosophy which has been passed on from sage to sage through untold ages — from Vivasvat, the sun, who told it to Manu, who in turn handed it down to rishis and seers until "the mighty art was lost"?* It is the core inspiration of sacred scripture, and the wisdom that we distill from daily experience. Theosophy has no creed, no dogma, no set of beliefs that must be accepted, because truth is not something beyond or outside us, but in fact is *within*. Nonetheless, it comprises a coherent body of teachings about man and nature that have been expressed in various ways in the sacred traditions of the world.

The modern theosophical movement began in the last quarter of the nineteenth century — a timely intervention, for the preceding decades had witnessed a radical upheaval in spiritual and intellectual thought. Theologians and scientists had been thrown into confusion and often bitter conflict after the publication in 1830–33 of Charles Lyell's *Principles of Geology*, which gave irrefutable evidence of earth's immense age. This was followed in 1859 by Charles Darwin's *The Origin of Species by Means of Natural Selection*, and *The Descent of Man* in 1871 which purported to trace man's origin to an ancient form which diverged from the Catarrhine monkey stock — arousing a controversy still very much alive today. Archaeology further revolutionized Western perspectives on man's spiritual history by revealing an Egyptian civilization of splendor and a Babylonian story of Noah and the Deluge that antedated the biblical one; moreover, the Orient, which until the 1780s had been a

---

*Cf. *Bhagavad-Gītā* 4:1–3 (Judge recension, p. 23).

closed book to the Occident, now was beginning to emancipate Western thought with its rich philosophic treasures.

World consciousness was ripe for change: on the one hand, rampant materialism both in theology and science had a stranglehold on independent inquiry and, on the other, many people hungry to believe in the immortality of the soul were being led astray by the will-o'-the-wisp of spiritualistic phenomena. A cosmic vision of man and his role in the universe was sorely needed, one that would restore trust in divine law and offer meaningful explanation of the seemingly cruel injustices of earthly existence.

H. P. Blavatsky, a woman of extraordinary gifts powered by a fearless devotion to truth and to the eradication of the *causes* of human suffering, became the leading exponent for the modern theosophical movement. One of a long line of "transmitters" of the universal god-wisdom, she cast into the thought-atmosphere of the world electrifying ideas, innovative ideas, ideas which would revolutionize the thinking of mankind. Chief among these was that *we are a oneness.* She encouraged the investigation and study of the spiritual heritage of all peoples, in order to eradicate the conceit that any race or people is the "chosen one," has the only true religion and the one and only God. Even a casual examination of other belief systems broadens our horizons. It is a thrilling experience to discern the same golden thread running through every tradition, whether religious, philosophic, or so-called primitive; we feel at once a sympathy, an empathy, with all who hold or cherish these truths. This in itself makes for a oneness, a feeling of understanding, a linkage of destiny.

Under the guidance and inspiration of her teachers, HPB was helped to write *The Secret Doctrine* (1888). Using a number of Stanzas from the Book of Dzyan, drawn from "a very old book" not found in any modern library, she unfolds a magnificent panorama encompassing the genesis and evolutionary destiny of our solar system, earth, and its life-forms. She reminds us that we are not merely a body, with a soul and spirit added on. On the contrary, we are structured on the same pattern as the cosmos, a seven-principled entity, whose gamut of qualities ranges from the physical to the highly ethereal and divine.

Every human being is a copy in miniature of what suns or stars are — living divinities housed in temples of matter. We have as vast a pilgrimage behind us as ahead of us: a past filled with long cycles of experience through which the soul has matured to its present status, and a future of limitless possibilities during which we will evolve out of humanhood into the full glory of godhood. HPB makes no claim to having originated these teachings; rather, she was a transmitter in current language of "a select number of fragments" from the esoteric records.

Before beginning her commentary on the Stanzas of Dzyan, HPB invites us to consider a few "fundamental conceptions which underlie and pervade the entire system of thought" (1:13) on which the sacred science of antiquity and the world's religious and philosophical schools are founded. Reduced to essentials, these are:

1) That there is an eternal, omnipresent, immutable Principle which cannot be defined as it is "beyond the range and reach of thought," yet from It all life emanates or flows

forth. Theosophy has no name for this Principle except to call it THAT — the infinite, the uncreate, the rootless root, the cause without a cause. These phrases are merely an effort to describe the indescribable, the infinity of infinities, the boundless essence of divinity which we cannot define. In short, it posits that marvelous primordial essence which *Genesis* calls the darkness on the face of the deep — that darkness which was sparked into light when the 'elohīm breathed on the waters of Space.

2) That universes like "manifesting stars" appear and disappear in tidal flux and ebb, a rhythmic pulsation of spirit and matter, with every life-spark in the cosmos, from stars to atoms, pursuing the same cyclic pattern. There is continual birth and death, appearance and disappearance, of these "sparks of Eternity" as the rhythm of life brings forth ever new life forms for returning worlds: galaxies and suns, human beings, animals, plants, and minerals. All beings and things have their birth and death cycles, because birth and death are gateways of life.

3) That all souls, being at their heart the same in essence as the "Universal Over-Soul," are required to undergo the full cycle of imbodiments in material worlds in order to bring into active expression, by self-effort, their divine potentialities.

Why does divinity manifest so many times and in so many different forms? Every divine seed, every spark of God, every unit of life, must go through the great cycle of experience, from the most spiritual realms to the most material, in order to gain firsthand knowledge of every condition of being. It must learn by becoming every form, i.e., by imbodying in them as it pursues its course through the arc of matter.

Here's a vision to lift the heart: to *feel* that every human being is a necessary part of the cosmic purpose is to give dignity to our strivings, to the urge to evolve. The reason for this grand "cycle of necessity" is twofold: whereas we start as unself-conscious god-sparks, by the time we have experienced all there is to learn in every life form, not only shall we have awakened into fuller awareness the multitudes of atomic lives which serve as our bodies on the various planes, but we ourselves shall have become gods in our own right.

When we grasp the intimate relationship of these three postulates to ourselves, we come to see how all the other teachings flow forth from them; they are as keys to a larger understanding of reimbodiment, cycles, karma, what happens after death, the cause and relief of suffering, the nature of man and cosmos, the interplay of involution/evolution, and more — all the while the awakening soul is pursuing the eternal quest.

The theosophical philosophy is vast as the ocean: "unfathomable in its deepest parts, it gives the greatest minds their fullest scope, yet, shallow enough at its shores, it will not overwhelm the understanding of a child."* Even though its truths go deeply into cosmological intricacies, a beautiful simplicity runs through the whole: *oneness* is the golden key. We *are* our brothers, no matter what our racial, social, educational, or religious background. And this affin-

---

*William Q. Judge, *The Ocean of Theosophy*, p. 1.

ity is not limited to the human kingdom: it takes in every atomic life that is evolving as we are — all within the webwork of hierarchies that compose this pulsating organism we call our universe. Assuredly our great error has been to regard ourselves as discrete particles adrift in a hostile universe, rather than as god-sparks struck from the central hearth of Divinity — as intrinsically one in essence as the flame of the candle is one with the stellar fires in the core of our sun.

The ancient Mahāyāna Buddhist, with his penchant for metaphor, perhaps said it best: in Indra's heaven is a network of pearls disposed in such a way that when you look at one pearl you find all the other pearls imaged in it; everything in the world likewise is linked with and involved in every other thing, "in fact *is* everything else."* How is it that we humans, supposedly the most advanced of earth dwellers, have ignored for so long this beautiful fact, especially when there is scarcely a race or people, clan or tribe, from the remotest past to the present era which has not cherished the knowledge of it?

Of course, acceptance of the principle of universal brotherhood is relatively simple compared to *living* it. All of us have difficulty at times living harmoniously with ourselves, let alone with others. Perhaps a first step would be to accept ourselves, to be friends with the whole of our nature, recognizing that when we do so we are accepting our lower tendencies along with our higher potentialities. In this acceptance we automatically are accepting others, their frail-

---

*Cf. "Avataṃsaka-sūtra," *Japanese Buddhism*, pp. 109–10.

ties as well as their grandeur. This is brotherhood in action, for it dispels those subtle blockages that bar us from feeling we all are units of one human life-wave.

Already the theme of our oneness with nature has revolutionized present-day thinking and lifestyles. Once again we are beginning to see ourselves as participants in an ecosystem of cosmic dimension. We are discovering that we, the observers, measurably affect not only the object we are observing but the entire complement of evolving entities. Best of all, we are realizing, though not sufficiently as yet, that we are *one* humanity, and that what you or I do to help another benefits all, striking a resonant chord in the on-going symphony that together we are composing. Though the burden of our inhumanities is indeed heavy, the universe must rejoice over the slightest movement of compassion in the soul of even a single human being.

2

Evolution

WHO IS MAN? A GOD IN PROCESS of becoming or a biological sport, a chance production of life in a cosmos otherwise void of intelligent, sentient beings? How singular that we should have forgotten our lineage when we are sprung of the seed of divinity, our souls assigned each to its "native star," as Plato tells us in his *Timaeus* (§§41–2), and when there is not a single atom in the immensities of space but is a consciousness-point instinct with life and the will to grow. Have we forgotten that we are gods currently housed in human temples; that our destiny is linked with that of every other human being; that we are, in fact, participants together in a cosmic procession of unfoldment that bonds us equally with the atoms of our body as with the courses of the stars and, by that token, with the heart of Infinity? As G. de Purucker wrote:

> Life is endless, has neither beginning nor end; and a universe is in no wise different in essentials from a man. . . . Consider the stars and the planets: every one of them is a life-atom* in the cosmic body; every one of them is the organized dwelling place of a multitude of smaller life-atoms

---

*The monadic life or divine spark animating every atom within the cosmos.

which build up the brilliant bodies we see. Moreover, every sparkling sun which begems the skies was at one time a man, or a being equivalent to a human, possessing in some degree self-consciousness, intellectual power, conscience and spiritual vision, as well as a body. And the planets and the myriads of entities on the planets encircling any such cosmic god, any such star or sun, are now the same entities who in far bygone cosmic manvantaras [cycles of manifestation] were the life-atoms of that entity.
— *Fountain-Source of Occultism,* p. 112

There is thus an intimate and strongly forged relationship on all levels between galaxies and humans: if, according to astrophysics, the chemical atoms of our physical constitution are formed in the interior of stars, would not the life-atoms of our mind and spirit be kin to those of the gods who use stars for bodies? Out of the darkness of chaos and the void, the firmament of stars, sun, moon, and planets came forth — and man too, his body formed of the dust of stars, his spirit born of divinities who gave him life. To what else did the Qabbālāh refer when it depicted those who came after the divine dynasties as "shooting down like falling stars" to enshrine themselves "in the shadows" and inaugurate our present earth and its humanities.*

When the universe came into being, the human kingdom was only one of several families of monads (Gk *monas,* one, single), individual atoms of light or sparks of divinity, who entered realms of matter for a grand purpose. We endure throughout the manvantara or world cycle — not our bodies, not our minds, but in the monadic core of our

---

*Cf. *The Secret Doctrine* 2:487.

being which is stamped with our unique essence. It is this monadic essence that spans the cycles of births and deaths, that urges our reincarnating ego to incarnate again and again in order to evolve forth ever more of its intrinsic quality. In other words, because our divine monad has to gain experience firsthand, it periodically widens and deepens its perceptions by animating every life form of ethereal and material substance it encounters along its evolutionary route; all the while it sparks into ever fuller awareness the life-atoms of the many-faceted constitution it will use as its means of enrichment.

As monads, then, we have already evolved through many different phases of life, taking form ages ago in the mineral kingdom. When we exhausted the experiences of the mineral world, we imbodied as plants, in a variety of trees and flowers and, when we could no longer find adequate expression in the vegetable kingdom, our monads took birth life after life in the animal kingdom, in all kinds of animal bodies. Finally, the divine essence within us was ready to assume the responsibility of humanhood, and to *know* that we are thinking beings. Ignited by the flame of mind, we went forth as true humans, enlightened in part, and blinded in part by material desire.

In the beginning we had on "garments of light," as the Qabbālāh phrases it; but as we descended the arc of matter we put on heavier and heavier "coats of skin" until we all but obscured our light source. We were as exiles from our divine home, having forgotten who we were and what our purpose was. So involved had we become with outer things (and still are) that we identified ourselves and our hopes and dreams with externals rather than with the inner life.

According to the *Mahābhārata*, the great epic of India, we have just passed the halfway point of the life of Brahmā or, as the theosophic teachings express it, the lowest point of the evolutionary arc, and have begun the rise toward spirit. This means that as a life-stream of egos we have passed the nadir and have begun the process, however slow our progress may seem, of shedding our coats of blindness, of matter.

In coming down the evolutionary arc ("down" and "up" are used for lack of better words), of necessity we attracted to ourselves more and more material atoms in order to build bodies suitable to the ever more material worlds we would be living in. We see this happening on a small scale in each human life. A child-to-be instinctively draws to itself atoms of life, of energy, to build its body. As its mind begins to awaken, it eagerly seizes everything before it — not selfishly, but because it has to gather to itself the life-atoms it needs in order to grow. The drive to seize for itself continues until the body is adult — though the tendency often persists longer than it ought. If it does, the current of growth mentally and psychologically may become egocentric and selfish. The time will come, as the cycles fulfill their course, when the family of man, along with earth and its kingdoms, will have shed their physical bodies, revealing once again the garments of light in which they were originally clothed.

There is but one pattern in nature, one purpose in view: the quickening of matter with the flame of spirit. As long as the focus is on producing material vehicles, spirit is recessive, in the background. Once the work of building vehicles is over, the explosive energy of spirit assumes command, its radiating force intensified. We are all radioactive: atoms, rocks, humans, and stars. A supernova, in ejecting its matter-particles, releases a thunderous burst of light far into space; just so, every time we transmute the iron of our nature into the bright essence of spirit, we irradiate the thought-world far and wide. It may be only a gleam, unseen by ourselves, but light is light, and wherever it shines it illumines the darkness. When at length we reach the top of the evolutionary arc, we will have evolved from within our full potentialities. We will be as gods walking the earth, having learned everything this planet can teach us. The end of our earth-experience will have arrived, and we will pass into a long rest.

But not forever — there is continuous ebb and flux, endings and beginnings, the death of old worlds and old experiences and the bringing to birth of new worlds, new experiences. As the cycles proceed, our human life-wave or family of monads will seek imbodiment on other planets or spheres until we have mastered all there is to be known in our solar system. In the long distant future we humans will have become suns, each with its own family of beings, while our present sun perchance will be the temple of a still greater solar being. In fact, we are "constantly affecting the destiny of the suns and planets of the future," and when we in turn shall have become suns, "then the nebulae and the suns around us will be the evolved entities who now are our fellow human beings. Consequently, the karmic relations that we have with each other on earth . . . will most assuredly affect their destiny as well as our own."* An awesome intermeshing of karmic links among all families of monads — from atomic to stellar and beyond!

The implications are profound: just as we humans after long association with animals, plants, and minerals are intimately tied in with their life cycles (scarcely an unmixed blessing, so casually have we exploited our younger brothers), just so the gods, by virtue of their having lived and worked among us during our formative period, are bonded with us forever, their influence and destiny irrevocably linked with ours. Reciprocity of responsibility and of caring would seem to be a dominant motif in nature's economy.

Such a perspective offers a very different view of man and his origins from those held by creationists, who adhere to a literal interpretation of *Genesis*, and also by evolutionists, the majority of whom regard *Homo sapiens* as having evolved from simian or anthropoid stock. As is often the case, truth appears to lie somewhere in the middle. Along with most religions, theosophy is in accord with the concept that man and all the kingdoms are "imaged in the Divine" — a spark of godhood being the fount and origin of every life form. Theosophy equally recognizes the presence of an orderly evolutionary progression, from less to greater — not by chance, but moved by intelligent, conscious agencies.

Charles Darwin was a remarkably gifted man with a deep religious sense, yet with respect to his speculative theories, particularly that of man's origin, he was surprisingly unscientific in presenting his case that the human mam-

---

*G. de Purucker, *Fountain-Source of Occultism*, pp. 112–13.

malia *followed* the monkeys and apes on the ladder of stocks.* The genealogical tree from protozoon to man, when impartially examined, shows numerous gaps in the scale of beings — too many "missing links." There is no hard fossil evidence for claiming a "straight-line-of-descent" from amoeba through monkeys to apes to Homo sapiens.†

Penetrating questions continue to be asked. The caldron of debate is impelling "a growing number of evolutionary specialists to go back to the drawing board: to the fundamentals of patterns and forms of nature."‡ They are starting from scratch, letting the chips fall where they may, so that they disclose what is and expose what is not. It is not our purpose here to report on the several new evolutionary hypotheses or interpretations of fossil finds that are currently under examination. Suffice to note a provocative statement by the late Finnish paleontologist, Björn Kurtén:

> Man did not descend from the apes. It would be more correct to say that apes and monkeys descended from early ancestors of man. The distinction is real: in the traits under consideration, man is primitive, apes and monkeys are specialized. — *Not From the Apes,* p. vii

This statement, as far as it goes, accords with the theosophic model, although that expounded by HPB and Purucker goes a good deal further. They maintain that the simians and apes are offshoots or descendants of man as the

---
* *The Descent of Man,* p. 155.
† Cf. Francis Hitching, *The Neck of the Giraffe: Where Darwin Went Wrong,* chapter 8, "Monkey business," pp. 199-224; also Eldredge and Tattersall, *The Myths of Human Evolution,* pp. 45-6.
‡ Hitching, p. 221.

result of a series of miscegenations, that is, mating of humans with animals; and that this occurred during the very early stages of humanity's racial experience, before the line of demarcation between human and animal stocks had become sharply drawn.

In *Man in Evolution,* a critique of the evolutionary theories that scientists since Darwin had propounded through the 1930s, Purucker analyzed the biological and anatomical evidence and showed that the physical form of man is beyond doubt far more primitive than that of the simians or other primates. As scientists have never found any anatomical characteristic to go backwards, but always forwards, obviously the most primitive features are the oldest; and as the bodies of monkeys and apes in significant ways are more specialized or evolved anatomically than man's body is, they must have come *after* man.

Rather than looking for fossil links, Purucker suggested that the real missing link in scientific theory is that of *consciousness,* the dynamic element behind the evolution of forms, human or other; further, that man was the origin, the parent and source of all species lower than himself. In brief, he takes man back to some prototype or original parent when the human stock had a semi-ethereal or astral form, from which over the ages many cells were cast off. These cast-off cells later developed along their individual lines to form the lower stocks.

It is ironic that since the publication of *The Descent of Man* most scientists along with the general public have taken Darwin's hypotheses as *facts,* instead of regarding them, as he had hoped, as *theories* to be tested and proved or disproved in the light of further investigation. The result has been to consolidate the materialistic view of life, rendering a grave disservice, particularly by the notion that we are merely evolved apes. Rightfully the creationists object to this, but their vision of man is equally limited by their dogmatic stance. We need to visualize ourselves as we really are — divinities who have been animating all manner of bodies for many aeons. Certainly in earlier imbodiments we — as monads — no doubt used a fish form, a reptile form, and a bird form before we imbodied in a mammal form. And if indeed we did use an apelike form in an earlier round of experience, this does not mean that we descended from the apes *in this present cycle.* The distinction, while subtle, is an important one to note.

Some anthropologists and paleontologists, in an endeavor to solve the many anomalies in current evolutionist theories, have suggested the likelihood of there being intelligent agencies behind the evolution of all species. They reason there must be some directing influence protecting and guiding the intricate and highly organized lower forms of life. Even so, they cannot account for the sudden marked changes that occurred in the human stock. What mysterious factor, they ask, precipitated the extraordinary leap in consciousness from that of animal to a creative, artistic, and original thinker? What happened?

3

The Quickening of Mind

TRADITIONS ALL OVER THE GLOBE describe an event of titanic import which occurred millions of years ago: the quickening of mind in childlike humanity. Where before we as a race had been dreamlike and without goal, now we were afire with the vigor of self-conscious thought, of choice, and the will to evolve. Legend and myth, scripture and temple preserve the record of this wondrous transition from mindlessness to self-awareness, from Eden-innocence to knowledge and responsibility — all due to the intervention of advanced beings from higher spheres who wrought within us "a living mind . . . and new mastery of thought."*

In the Purāṇas of India, for example, and also in the *Bhagavad-Gītā* and other sections of the *Mahābhārata*, are a number of references to our divine ancestors being descended from seven or ten "mind-born sons of Brahmā." They go under different names, but all are mind-born, *mānasa*, "thinking" (from *manas*, "mind," derived from the Sanskrit verb *man*, "to think, to reflect"). Occasionally they are called *mānasaputras*, "sons of mind"; more often *agnishvāttas*, those who have tasted of *agni*, "fire"; also

---

*Prometheus Bound, Aeschylus, trans. Gilbert Murray, lines 445–6.

barhishads, those who sit on *kuśa* grass for meditative or ceremonial purposes; or they are referred to simply as *pitṛis*, "fathers" — terms that preserve the tradition that solar and lunar fathers, progenitors, gave mind and the power to choose to early humanity so that we humans might pursue our further evolution with conscious intent.

The awakening of mind in an entire humanity could not have been accomplished by a single heroic deed; it must have taken hundreds of thousands, if not several million years to achieve. And the humans of that predawn period no doubt were as diverse as we are today: the most enlightened were probably few in number, the great majority of mankind being in the middle range of attainment, while some lacked the impetus to activate their potential. The coming of the light-bearers was indeed an act of compassion, yet it was destined also because of karmic links with humanity from previous world cycles.

Understandably, the unleashing of this new power among a humanity as yet undisciplined in the use of knowledge called for guides and mentors to point the way. Legends and traditions of many peoples relate that higher beings remained to teach, inspire, and foster aspiration as well as intellect. They imparted practical skills: navigation, star lore, metallurgy, and husbandry, herbal medicine, carding and spinning, and hygiene; also a love of beauty through the arts. More important than all else, they impressed deep within the soul memory of those early humans certain fundamental truths about ourselves and about the cosmos, to serve as an inner talisman for ensuing cycles.

In the West poets and philosophers for centuries have

elaborated on the legends surrounding Prometheus which the Greek poet Hesiod (8th century BC) recorded from very ancient sources. Among others, Aeschylus, Plato, Vergil, Ovid, and in more recent times Milton, Shelley, and others immortalized various facets of the tale. In his Dialogues Plato hints often of a wisdom beyond the myths he relates, and in his *Protagoras* (§320 ff) he tells of the confrontation of Epimetheus (Afterthinker) with his older brother Prometheus (Forethinker). When the cycle had come for "mortal creatures" to be formed, the gods fashioned them from the elements of earth and fire "in the interior of the earth," but before bringing them into the light of day they commissioned Epimetheus and Prometheus to apportion to each its proper qualities. Epimetheus offered to do the main work, leaving the inspection and approval to Prometheus.

All went well with respect to furnishing the animals with suitable attributes; but, alas, Epimetheus discovered he had used everything up, "and when he came to man, who was still unprovided [for], he was terribly perplexed." Prometheus had but one recourse, and that was to procure by stealth from the common workshop of Athena, goddess of the arts, and of Hephaestus, god of fire and craftsmanship, that which was needed to equip "man in his turn to go forth into the light of day." Off Prometheus sped to the forge of the gods where burned the everlasting fire of mind. Stealing an ember from the sacred hearth, he descended again to earth and quickened man's latent mind with the fire of heaven. Man the thinker was born: instead of being less qualified than the animals which Epimetheus had so well equipped, he now stood a potential god, conscious of his power, yet innately aware that from then on he would have to choose between good and evil, and *earn* the gift Prometheus had brought.

At first the youthful humans (ourselves) lived at peace, but in time many of us turned our mind-power to selfish ends and were "in process of destruction." Zeus, noting our plight, called Hermes and empowered him to go swiftly to earth and instill "reverence and justice" in every man and woman, so that all, and not merely a favored few, would share in the virtues. In short, we humans, however unequal in talent or opportunity, are equal in divine potential.

In myth form Plato transmits the beautiful truth that not only did Zeus sow within man the seed of immortality (see likewise *Timaeus* §41), but also, at the appointed hour, an ember of the mind-fire of the gods fructified that seed into self-conscious awareness of his divinity — the work of Prometheus, whose daring and sacrifice for the sake of humanity make him the noblest of heroes.

The third chapter of *Genesis*, when understood, tells the same story, with God warning Adam and Eve not to eat of the fruit of the tree of knowledge of good and evil, or they would die. But the serpent assures Eve that they "shall not surely die," for God — or rather gods, *'elohīm*, plural — know(s) that as soon as they do eat from it, their "eyes shall be opened, and [they] shall be as gods, knowing good and evil." They did eat, and they did "die" — as a race of mind-innocent children — and became truly human, became *as gods, knowing good and evil.* And here we are, gods in our inmost being, though largely unaware of this since memory of this momentous truth has faded.

Turning to the same story in the Stanzas of Dzyan of *The Secret Doctrine* we find:

> The great Chohans called the Lords of the Moon, of the airy bodies. "Bring forth men, men of your nature. Give them their forms within. She [Mother Earth] will build coverings without. Males-females will they be. Lords of the Flame also . . ."
> They went each on his allotted land: seven of them each on his lot. The Lords of the Flame remain behind. They would not go, they would not create. — 2:16

Thus it came about that seven times seven creatures were fashioned, shadowy, and each after his own kind. Yet the beings with mind had still to be born. The Fathers each provided what they had, the Spirit of the Earth as well. It was not enough: "Breath needs a mind to embrace the Universe; 'We cannot give that,' said the Fathers. 'I never had it,' said the Spirit of the Earth." Early man remained an "empty senseless" being.

"How did the Mānasa, the Sons of Wisdom, act?" They spurned the earlier forms as unfit; but when the third race was produced, "the powerful with bones," they said, "We can choose, we have wisdom." Some entered the shadowy (astral) forms; others "projected the Spark"; still others "deferred till the fourth" race. Those in whom the mind-spark entered fully became enlightened, sages, the leaders and guides of average humanity in whom the spark had been but partially projected. Those in whom the spark had not been projected, or burned too low, were irresponsible; they mated with animals and bred monsters. The Sons of Wisdom repented: "This is Karma," they said, because they had refused to create. "Let us dwell in the others. Let us teach them better, lest worse should happen. They did. . . . Then all men became endowed with Manas [mind]."

Thus did the third race produce the fourth, whose inhabitants "became tall with pride." As the cycle of evolution rapidly moved toward its lowest point in the arc of material descent, temptations multiplied. It is recorded that a fearsome battle took place between the Sons of Light and the Sons of Darkness. "The first great waters came. They swallowed the seven great islands." The Sons of Light took birth among the incoming fifth race — our own — to give it the needed spiritual impetus, and "taught and instructed it."*

The igniting of our intellectual faculties was a climactic moment in human evolution. It quickened our awareness of everything: we became conscious of who and what we were — self-conscious. Knowledge gave us power: power to choose, to think, and to act — wisely and unwisely. It gave us the ability to love and to understand others. It stimulated the yearning to evolve and expand our capacities. In the process it gave us the greatest challenge of all: the awakening of our powers for both beneficence and maleficence, culminating in a contest between the light and dark forces in ourselves. When we multiply this by several billion human souls, we easily understand why there has been and still is a continual conflict of wills.

During the third great racial cycle or root-race, the mānasaputras, who united their mind-essence with the latent mind of those early humans, remained with us as

---

*The Secret Doctrine 2:16–21, Stanzas III–XII.

divine instructors. Inevitably, however, there came a time when these higher beings retired so that the young humanity could evolve and develop on its own. They withdrew from our immediate presence, but they never withdrew their love and protective concern, any more than a mother and father ideally will ever stop loving their children. The wise parent learns that the greatest gift he can give his children is his trust in them that they can make it on their own. That is what the mānasaputras did for us; and what our god-essence is continuing to do for the human portion of ourselves.

In fact, *we* are mānasaputras, although in its higher reaches mind is not as yet fully manifest in us. Nonetheless, the truths the mind-born sons implanted in our soul-memory remain an intrinsic part of ourselves. It is for the purpose of consciously reestablishing contact with this inborn wisdom-knowledge that we come again and again to earth: to rediscover who we truly are, companions of stars and galaxies and fellow humans as surely as we are of our brothers of field, ocean, and sky — one flowing consciousness, from our parent star to crystals and diamonds, and further, to the tiny lives that animate the world of the atom. Nor do we overlook the several classes of elemental or primary beings who maintain the integrity of the elements of aether, fire, air, water, and earth.

It may seem strange to think of ourselves as one flowing consciousness, yet this is just what we are. We see our human self as a separate unit when in fact it is only a cell, we might say, of the loftier being in which humanity is living and having its conscious evolutionary experience. Separateness is an illusion. There is an interconnection among all nature's families — in the sense that all beings are sacrificing a little of themselves for the benefit of the kingdoms above and below them. There is an interchange of helpfulness constantly going on that we might intuit more often could we *feel* our oneness with all. Along with a constant interchange of life-atoms and of energies of many kinds, there is also an intermeshing of karma among all of nature's kingdoms. Indeed, we have the mineral, plant, and animal kingdoms within us, and the elemental kingdoms as well, and we also have the god kingdoms within us, because we are gods in human form. We too often overemphasize our seeming separateness.

Today an astonishing array of evidence is confirming that consciousness is *one* and that while it manifests in different ways in stone, plant, animal, and human, it is one flowing river of life. Experiments with plants, for example, suggest plant sensitivity to human thoughts and to music. If there is reciprocity of vibration, both positive and negative, between humans and plants, it surely exists among our own species. The continuous interchange of thought-energies, of thought-atoms, among us is not limited to the human kingdom or to our planet. When we reflect on the living network of magnetic and soul force between ourselves and every aspect of the cosmic organism we call our universe, we sense something of the magnitude of our responsibility. If we could view all that occurs in our personal circumstances, in our social and communal relationships, from this perspective, from the eye of our immortal self, we would transform every aspect of human living.

4

Reincarnation

YOU AND I ARE ON A VAST PILGRIMAGE of exploration of the cosmos. We entered it aeons ago, impelled by the divine spark within us to seek experience, to gain knowledge of ourselves and of the truths of nature. In order to grow, to evolve, we took on bodies of gradually increasing materiality so that we might learn firsthand what this whole earth experience is about. Though we may not fully realize it, as we are often at cross-purposes with ourselves and with our circumstances, we as a humanity are beginning to awaken, to shake off our cloaks of matter, of blindness, and to glimpse a little behind the veil of appearances to the reality of the godhead that gave us birth. And that godhead is both our Self and our Father in heaven.

Reincarnation offers a sound and compassionate perspective on the totality of our lives. What other theory can compare with the ennobling concept that human beings, in concert with all of nature's kingdoms, are evolving participants in a timeless cosmic process — a process that includes a succession of births and deaths in and for every life form? It encompasses both the infinitely large and the infinitely minute. Who are we? Where did we come from, and why? And what kind of future may we expect, as individuals and as a species? There is a great deal of confusion in our current thinking, largely because we have alienated ourselves from our source, our god-essence. We need to know with certainty that our roots go deeper than this one life, and that a part of us endures beyond death. We need to find meaning in suffering and behind the frightening injustices inflicted upon children, animals, and millions of innocent victims of ruthless crimes and senseless accidents when there is no apparent cause in this life.

Solid knowledge today about these matters that ought most to concern us is appallingly slight, not because it is unavailable — there is a fund of teaching and practical wisdom in the world's religions, in myth, legend, aboriginal tradition, and fairy tale — but because we have forgotten how to apply the universal keys that are waiting to be used intelligently and with altruistic motive.

The concept of reincarnation is, of course, very old, and the cyclic return of the human soul for learning purposes and expansion of awareness was as widely understood throughout the ancient pagan world as it still is in much of the Orient. Several early Church Fathers, versed in Platonic and Pythagorean thought, accepted it, among them Origen, who wrote of the soul's preexistence and of its taking birth again in a body according to its merits and former deeds; and, further, that ultimately, when bodies and material things will suffer ruin and disappear, all spirits will be united in one.

For centuries these and other doctrinal theses of Origen were considered as having been officially condemned and banned by the Fifth Ecumenical Council called by Emperor

Justinian and held in Constantinople in 553 AD. Careful scrutiny of the record, however, shows that neither Origen nor his beliefs were aired at any session of the Council. It was at an extra-conciliary meeting held prior to the Council that fifteen Anathemas were pronounced against Origen and his teachings, the first of which reads:

> If anyone assert the fabulous pre-existence of souls, and shall assert the monstrous restoration which follows from it: let him be anathema.*

It seems incomprehensible to us today that a teaching as broadly accepted and as logical and spiritually satisfying as reincarnation should have been withdrawn from public knowledge and held under ecclesiastical wraps for nearly 1,500 years. One cannot help wondering what the history of the Occident might have been had the concept of reincarnation remained a vivifying element in the Christian message. Providentially, although it was taboo to preach from the pulpit the doctrine of the soul's rebirth, the immortal song of bards and poets could not be silenced, and when the Renaissance came, philosophers joined poets in speaking and writing openly of intimations of an earlier life or lives. Later, Transcendentalists on both sides of the Atlantic powerfully affirmed their support of this transforming idea, this doctrine of hope and consolation.

Against the background of cosmic cycles, the birth and death of stars, and the annual renewal of earth and all its kingdoms, reincarnation is seen as the human mode of

---

Reincarnation: The Phoenix Fire Mystery, comp. and ed. by Joseph Head and Sylvia Cranston, p. 159 ff.

the universal process of Divinity manifesting in terrestrial spheres — the Word made flesh of Christian tradition — the Logos seeking imbodiment after imbodiment in numberless forms for the purpose of bringing into activity the seed-logos dwelling within the inmost essence of every entity. Is this not what the human adventure is all about: to *become* that which we feel so deeply we really are?

Many have the feeling as their life goes by that there is so much still unfinished, so much that could be expressed were there more time. Our body grows older, but *we* don't. How natural, then, for the evolving ego to return to earth after a rest period to continue inscribing new pages in its Book of Life. Everything works together, smaller cycles meshing with larger cycles to enable the fullest growth possible for each entity in its appropriate time and place. To this end nature provides ever new forms so that her myriad children — each a living being, a consciousness-center, a monad at its heart — may pursue their evolutionary goals.

The cells of our body are born and die many times within our life span, yet we retain our physical integrity; family and friends know us even though our entire complement of molecules, cells, and atoms are continually being renewed. It's a miracle: the years pass, our hair turns white, but we are always recognizable as ourselves. And why? Because there is a substratum of form, an astral or model body on which the physical is built; and that astral model is itself but a reflection of an inner model. You can go further and further inward until you come to the life-seed, the logos within every person, the light of the Logos which "lighteth every man that cometh into the world."

A number of Buddhist texts refer to *svabhāva,* "self-becoming": that what is inherent in the invisible essence of an entity will "self-become," that is, will unfold that essence in accordance with its own distinctive pattern. In *Genesis,* God ('elohīm) commanded the earth to bring forth grass and herbs and the fruit tree, "whose seed is in itself," each after its kind (1:11–12). Paul in his first letter to the Corinthians (15:38–41) also speaks of God (*theos*) giving to every seed its own body: "there is one glory of the sun," another glory of the moon, and another of the stars, "for one star differeth from another star in glory."

The basic idea of svabhāva ties in with the Vedantic concept of *sūtrātman*: *sūtra*, "thread, cord," and *ātman*, "self." This "thread-self" or radiant essence not only links every portion of our multifaceted being, from the divine to the physical, but also links us with the totality of our past. How many lives must we have lived? We don't know; but if we believe at all in the immortality of spirit, we have a sense of an infinity of experience both behind as well as ahead of us. Every human being therefore has a rich reserve of unexpended force within (for good and ill) that at some time in this life or in lives to come will seek outlet; the entirety of our karma could not find expression within the brief interval of seventy or eighty years, or of twenty.

At every moment we are the totality of our past and the promise of the future that is to be. Such a perspective gives a feeling of continuity, an assurance that all that we have been remains *in essence,* incised on the memory tablets of eternity, on the seed-logos of our being, waiting for the precise karmic circumstances to find active expression.

HPB speaks of sūtrātman, the "thread of radiance," as being imperishable throughout the great world cycle and disappearing or dissolving only in nirvana, the great rest period, after which it will reemerge "*in its integrity on the day when the Great Law calls all things back into action.*"* This opens up a marvelous vista. Just as Jesus told the Jews in the temple, "Before Abraham was, I am" (*John* 8:58), so humanity as a life-wave of monads was there as essences, particles of divinity, of life, of consciousness, awaiting the cyclic moment when the universe was to come forth again in a new birth, a new flowering. When it manifests, we do also, numberless seed-logoi, seeds of life, each with its distinctive character or svabhāva; and at the close of its active cycle, when it enters another rest period, we do likewise, for we are part of and one with all — there is no separation. Yet every spark of godhood, though reabsorbed into non-being when the drama of a life-period ends, retains its inherent mark of selfhood. This is *its* mark, and no one else's: the whole purpose of its being is to develop its characteristic essence to the full.

How does this vast picture of reimbodiment of worlds and human beings and all life forms relate to the scientific views of heredity? Obviously, physical mechanisms for heredity exist, but could the body be formed without any connection with the part of us that outlasts many deaths? In his writings, G. de Purucker goes into the subject of reincarnation extensively, emphasizing that the process of rebirth starts long before the moment of conception. When

---

**The Secret Doctrine* 2:80.

an individual feels the urge to be born again on earth, the reincarnating element is attracted magnetically to the father and mother to be, and begins to form a *laya*-center* or focus of attraction for its former life-atoms, physical and other.

Once conception takes place, it directs the building of its body within the mother's womb. The mother is the protector, the channel, and nurturer, as is also the father, for both parents share in providing protection to the growing child, which in a very real sense extends beyond its physical compass. As the incoming entity gradually forms its new physical vehicle by gathering life-atoms that formerly belonged to it, so the body will inevitably bear the stamp of the child-to-be. In due course a child is born.†

Our DNA contains a record of all our past. It couldn't be otherwise. That physically every human being has a genetic code distinctly its own confirms the theosophic teaching that each of us *is* his own karma; and, further, that our present character and circumstances in this life are not the outcome of only one previous life's karma, but of the karma that we have engendered for kalpas beyond number. We are ageless sparks of eternity, with a beginningless and endless pattern of destiny that has been in the making for aeons. In every atom of our being, from the physical to the divine, we are stamped with the memory essences of what we have been and aspired to be. Our individual DNA is the physical record of our inner explorations, adventures,

---

*The mystical point where an energy or thing vanishes from one plane to manifest on a higher or lower plane.

†Consult *The Esoteric Tradition* and *Fountain-Source of Occultism* by G. de Purucker.

progress — and of our future too, because we are the future in seed.

In reality the reincarnation of a human being is primarily a spiritual event. Life is sacred at all times. It does not start with conception; its manifestation on this plane may begin then, but *life* is a continuing process. We have confused our values largely because we know so little about who we are. We think that we as parents own our children and that because sperm and ovum meet and an embryo forms within the body of a mother, that the mother makes the child. That is not true. The living entity that is animating a fetus is not a new creation, freshly minted by God for this life only; rather, it represents a reentry into earth-life of a returning ego or soul that has had a long series of lives reaching back into eternity's past. In this context, indeed, abortion is highly questionable, except to save the life of the mother. Who are we to decide to cut short the soul's experience in midstream? We cannot cut it off completely, but we can and do interrupt its process of incarnation — fortunately only for a time, because the returning soul will try again and again, if need be, until it finds an opening for rebirth.

Undoubtedly there are instances when the decision is extremely difficult: victims of rape, of willful assault and incest, draw deeply upon our sympathies. Nevertheless, the fact remains: a child who has been begun has as much right for a chance on this earth as any other, painful though the circumstances may be for it and all concerned. None of us knows the interlinkings of karma that impel that child to seek just those parents and those conditions which, if worked through intelligently and with love, will benefit child and parents alike.

Paradoxically, we know too much and too little about the mystery of birth. Modern technology enables parents to see the growing embryo and discover perchance that their baby will be badly crippled or mentally handicapped. The thought instinctively comes: wouldn't it be kinder to end the baby's life before it is born, so as to save it and its parents needless suffering? It is a harrowing decision; but with the larger perspective that a knowledge of reincarnation and karma yields, the question remains: should we not give the benefit to life rather than to death? We have to distinguish between the immortal element and the body. Oftentimes physical handicaps are of signal import for soul development; we are not trained or wise enough to comprehend the inner purpose behind an incoming ego's choice of a mental or physical abnormality. Isn't it conceivable that the reincarnating ego might "choose" the karma of a defective vehicle for purposes beyond our knowing?

When we trust that life is inherently just and compassionate, regardless of appearances and seeming injustices and cruelties that beset people all over the world, we know that no child is born to a family or into circumstances where it does not belong. In principle, it is fairly simple to agree to this. However, if our higher self invites into our home a child who is severely impaired, mentally, physically, or psychologically, it may be difficult at first not to feel we have been cheated. There are thousands, probably millions of these "special" children, but this by no means indicates they are *spiritually* handicapped. If we can take the long-range view we will know that this little one has chosen us as parents, to love and nurture it through its present ordeal. To give love and tenderness unconditionally calls for a magnanimity of soul that accepts the present karma as a gift. The wonder is that many parents, after the initial shock, are doing just this, drawing upon resources of love and resilience they were unaware they had.

These teachings about death, rebirth, and the continuum of the consciousness-center have appeal because they apply directly to many aspects of our life and our relationships. We are many-splendored beings, with a karmic history stretching far into the past and with an ever receding horizon of opportunity before us. We can dare to believe in ourselves and in humanity's future. Inwardly, whatever the individual or global karma, we have an ancestry of soul experience that has been aeons in the making, giving assurance of unimagined richness of quality and power yet to be unfolded in future cycles.

5

Death: A Doorway to Light

HOW WE THINK ABOUT OURSELVES — whether we have but one lifetime in which to flower, or whether we have a limitless future in which to cultivate our hidden strengths and talents — will have a profound effect on our outlook on life. People are yearning for confirmation of their intuition that there is a compassionate order, a harmonious and just purpose behind everything.

Every human being knows death among family and friends, prolonged illness, or the grievous distress that comes when a child or friend becomes a psychological or mental casualty. A philosophy that takes in reincarnation, that emphasizes individual moral responsibility and the promise of ever-continuing growth in love and wisdom, helps enormously. Then when death comes, suddenly or after long waiting, it doesn't hit us totally unprepared, with an almost terrifying sense of betrayal, as though fate had dealt us a cruel blow. We wouldn't be human if we didn't feel the loss deeply, and the loneliness, but there come also in the quiet an inner calm and the profound assurance that "all is well."

Death is not the tragic ending of a life; it is truly an open doorway to light — both for those journeying to the "other shore," and for those of us here who must carry on with our lives. How little we know of those mysterious regions into which our consciousness enters nightly in sleep and for a far longer interval after the death of the body. Yet we follow these circulatory routes as though drawn magnetically to them, much as birds migrate thousands of miles by magnetic currents. In like manner we humans unerringly find our way back to earth time and again after migrations lasting perhaps hundreds, even thousands, of years in nature's interior realms.

Sleep we accept gracefully, thankful for our nightly rest; but death, we feel, is different. Intellectually we may recognize it as nature's way of restoring her life forces, that the release of the soul from an ailing or aged body is a boon, and that without periodic changes of form there could be no continuity of inner growth. Still, the coming of death is always a shock: we feel held by a power vaster than we can comprehend; we sense its irrevocability, that all hope is gone of sharing the unspoken thought. Yet mercifully we are sustained by a profound peace, an inflow of strength, an atmosphere of quiet assurance that the bonds linking us with those we love are as immortal as the heart of Being.

We tend to think of our life on earth as of absolute importance, when in reality it represents only a part of our unfolding destiny. Like the Aśvattha tree of India, which is said to grow with its roots in heaven and its branches and leaves reaching downwards, we human beings are rooted in our divine monad whose light is reflected in our spiritual intelligence, our mental/emotional nature, and even in our physical body.

To comprehend more clearly what happens to us after death we need first to understand something of the several elements that make us up, and the role they play both during our lives and after we die. Paul's division of man into spirit, soul, and body is basic and useful in relation to other systems of thought, which classify man variously as being composed of four, five, seven, or even ten facets or principles. These facets of man's nature are not isolated one from another. In the sevenfold system, for example, each facet is itself sevenfold and contains an aspect of all the others. We could as easily adopt a fivefold division, into monads of descending quality with their corresponding sheaths or vehicles of expression; or again, a fourfold enumeration, as the Qabbālāh does, three "breaths" of gradually more material quality, all manifesting through a "shell," our physical body.

Using the sevenfold division as generally followed in theosophical writings, the principles (with their Sanskrit names) are listed, starting with the highest:

Divinity — *ātman*, "self," our immortal monad;

Spirit — *buddhi*, "awakened intelligence," the veil of ātman: the faculty of perception attained in full by a buddha;

Mind — *manas*, dual in function: higher manas united with the highest two principles constitutes the spiritual individuality (ātma-buddhi-manas); lower manas attracted toward kāma, the "desire" principle, manifests as the ordinary personality (manas-kāma);

Desire — *kāma*, "love, desire"; when influenced by the higher mind (buddhi-manas), it manifests as aspiration; when utilized by the personality (manas-kāma), without any influence from the higher element, it may manifest in aggressive selfishness or uncontrolled appetites, often of a destructive nature;

Life-force — *prāṇa*, the "vital breaths," listed as five, seven, or more in number, that circulate through our constitution and maintain physical life;

Astral or Model Body — *liṅga-śarīra*, the "sign or character body"; the model or astral matrix on which the physical body is built;

Physical Body — *sthūla-śarīra*, the "coarse or bulky body," the physical vehicle or instrument which allows the complete sevenfold entity to manifest.

To understand the relation of these seven facets of our being to our afterdeath experiences, we have first to recognize that death does not come merely because the body is tired or worn out. Death occurs primarily because the higher part is drawing the soul to itself and the upward pull is so strong that the body cannot withstand it. The life is being indrawn, as it were, for the larger purposes of the soul. Birth and death are gateways of *life* — episodes in the maturation of the reincarnating element and hence both processes, death and birth, are in the final analysis impulsed from our divine source.

The many stories of individuals who have almost drowned, been critically ill, or pronounced "dead" and then revived, demonstrate the manifold nature of the human constitution, and that it is possible for the body to be left quiescent while the soul/mind/consciousness is momentarily withdrawn. Some have experienced the feeling of being alive and floating above the body, seeing it lying below. A few have later recalled exactly what the doctors and nurses said and did during their apparent death; most of them tell of seeing the events of their life flash swiftly by in review. Such near-death experiences are a graphic confirmation of the theosophical teaching concerning the "panoramic vision" which the mind/soul undergoes preceding its release into the afterdeath journey. Not all who undergo a near-death experience are aware of anything out of the ordinary having happened to them, but those who do retain some memory of what they have "seen" usually return with a strong determination to make the rest of their life worthy of this second chance.

In sleep the golden cord of life remains intact between all parts of our constitution, while in death the cord is snapped. In near death the cord is *not* severed, so that even if there is a more or less prolonged withdrawal, the connecting link between the principles is not broken. This means that the individual can, and usually does, reanimate his body and a seeming miracle occurs: a person thought dead returns to life. Had the cord been broken, death would have supervened.

Theosophical writings speak of two, sometimes three panoramic visions of varying intensity: the one experienced by the dying during the final moments of physical life and continuing for a while after physical death; a second, much fainter, occurring just before slipping into a heavenly dream state (*devachan*); and a third, upon leaving the dream state on the return journey to earth.* This allows the individual

---

*Cf. H. P. Blavatsky, *The Key to Theosophy*, pp. 162–3, and G. de Purucker, *Fountain-Source of Occultism*, pp. 549–54.

to "see" without distortion the simple justice of all that occurred during the life just ended, to enter its heavenly dream state in peace, and upon its return to earth to have a swift preview in broad outline of what is to be, before the curtain of forgetfulness drops.

When death finally comes and the soul is released from its bodily chains, the ray from the divine monad is withdrawn to its parent star, while our spiritual monad journeys among the planetary spheres. As for the body, its atoms disperse and go to their respective realms in nature where they follow their own circulations. This constitutes our "first" death. After a brief period of unconsciousness in what is called the desire-world (*kāma-loka*), the human soul enters a temporary purgation state during which it stands unmasked before its higher self and sees the fairness of all it had experienced. A separation process of shorter or longer duration, depending upon the karma previously generated, leads to a "second" death, when all that is heavy and material in the character drops away, freeing the finer essences of the reincarnating ego to be absorbed by the spiritual monad. For most of us — average human beings who are neither very good nor very bad — our passage in kāma-loka will be gone through with relative ease.

After the second panoramic vision during the "second" death, the reincarnating ego enters its devachan — the Elysian Fields of the Greeks — wherein it experiences over and over in a dreamlike state the fulfillment of its noblest thoughts and aspirations. The repetition of these idealized dreams has the beneficial by-product of leaving an impress on the soul toward the higher life, the atmosphere of which carries over into the succeeding life on earth. Meanwhile the spiritual monad, bearing within it the dreaming ego-soul, journeys among the planetary spheres for its own higher adventures. The old Latins made effective use of the epitaph to perpetuate the ancient knowledge: *dormit in astris,* "he sleeps among the stars"; *gaudeat in astris,* "he rejoices among the stars"; and *spiritus astra petit,* "the spirit flies to the stars."

When the energies that have made devachan possible are exhausted, a third panoramic vision occurs, a swift preview in bold strokes, not in detail — a momentary glimpse so that the incoming soul may sense the justice and the compassion in the karmic circumstances that it will meet. As it turns earthward, it attracts from the great reservoir of nature those life-atoms it had built into itself in the past; with them it re-forms the souls and bodies it will use in the life to come. These life-atoms are drawn to each of us because they belong to us; in previous lives we had left our seal on all the lives composing every facet of our constitution.

These ideas may seem abstract when we are struck down with grave illness, and are able to do little about it. There may be certain remedial measures we can take, but where there is no known cure, we have to try to meet the experience with the best grace and courage we can summon. If we have a feeling for the long view and are convinced that there is a divine purpose to every life, this in itself is a tremendous aid in meeting such a crisis. Particularly is it a help when we must stand by and see another go through his private hell that we can do very little to relieve. Even more so when the young are hit with life-threatening illness and find their lives plunged into confusion. Naturally, the person who is faced with early death has a painful process of adjustment to go through, and equally so have those who love him or her.

Many people are having to meet just these circumstances, and a knowledge of reincarnation lends dignity to living and to dying. We realize that how we live when we are twenty or forty or sixty influences the quality of our death, our afterlife, as well as our future incarnations. If we can share something of this larger picture with our loved ones, they are better able to work with their karma and do as Marcus Aurelius enjoined: "Now your remaining years are few. Live them, then, as though on a mountaintop."* There is a dignity in the human soul that comes into its own in these hours of trial. Even where there are very difficult patches to go through, it helps immeasurably to know that our lives are a natural part of the destiny each of us has been weaving since the dawn of time, which has been preparing us for just this moment. It is mutually healing to be able to talk quietly and openly or silently commune with those who are dying; not only do they find deep relief, but we ourselves share in the process in a most sacred way.

**Meditations*, bk. 10, §15, trans. Staniforth, p. 157.

6

Remembering and Forgetting Past Lives

MOST OF US DO NOT REMEMBER our past lives or what happens between earth lives. Greek mythology tells us that we drink of the waters of Lethe — Unmindfulness, Forgetfulness — which blots out sufficient memory of our past so that we enter earth life with a clean slate on which to inscribe the thoughts, emotions, and deeds that will determine the quality of the life to be. We have each been writing our individual Book of Destiny for ages, and in this incarnation we are writing another page or chapter. If we had a detailed memory of all that we had inscribed in the past or, on the other hand, knew in precise detail the series of events that may occur in the future, we should be severely handicapped. The full memory of ourselves — and of others — would be too heavy a burden.

We are not yet wise or strong enough to go without drinking of Lethe's waters. Were it possible, three difficulties would arise: first, we should be burdened by past failures, for they would hang like an albatross around our neck; secondly, we should be burdened by past successes because in all probability they would engender pride and vanity; thirdly, if we had not forgotten anything, we probably would also remember the failures and successes of others, and this could be damaging indeed.

People have always tried to peer into the past and future, looking for counsel and insight. In ancient days the Greeks sought guidance from oracles at Delphi, Trophonius, Mount Olympus, and other sacred shrines. If the heart was pure, the mind disciplined, the answers received reawakened inner sources of wisdom. What lines of communication existed then between gods and humans? Today we seek guidance as of old, seek light upon the vexing problems of fear and despair which long ages of folly, ignorance, and greed have precipitated upon us in the present confusion of ideals.

Alas, the woods are full of quack oracles, counterfeit priests and priestesses who, professing communion with the divine, sell their unholy wares to the foolish and emotion-blinded. Nonetheless, communion between god and man is and always will be possible, for the power to tap the secret wellspring of truth is resident within the soul. Knowledge of such, however, is reserved for those who consort with Nous, the Knower within, personified as Mnemosyne, Goddess of Memory. Who is this goddess and what is her function?

Mnemosyne, mother of the Muses, is the counterpart of Nous, whose duty it is to arouse Psyche, the soul, to recollection of truth so that, remembering her divine origin, she will at last claim union with Nous. Among the relics of the Orphic mysteries, recovered from tombs in Crete and southern Italy, are eight small and very thin gold-leaf tablets finely inscribed in Greek characters. One of these found near Petelia, in the environs of Strongoli, tells of two wellsprings near the entrance to the Underworld: the fount of Lethe or Oblivion (unnamed) on the left, that of Mnemosyne or Memory to the right:

> Thou shalt find to the left of the House of Hades a Well-spring,
> And by the side thereof standing a white cypress.
> To this Well-spring approach not near.
> But thou shalt find another by the Lake of Memory,
> Cold water flowing forth, and there are Guardians before it.
> Say: "I am a child of Earth and of Starry Heaven;
> But my race is of Heaven (alone). This ye know yourselves.
> And lo, I am parched with thirst and I perish. Give me quickly
> The cold water flowing forth from the Lake of Memory."
> And of themselves they will give thee to drink from the holy Well-spring,
> And thereafter among the other Heroes thou shalt have lordship. . . .*

In this hymn the Orphic candidate is warned against imbibing the waters of Lethe. In another account by Pausanias, 2nd-century AD Greek traveler and geographer, the candidate drinks from the well of Lethe in order to "forget all that he has been thinking of hitherto."† Thereafter he partakes of the waters of Mnemosyne, that he may

---

*See Jane Harrison, *Prolegomena to the Study of the Greek Religion*, "Critical Appendix on the Orphic Tablets" by Prof. Gilbert Murray, pp. 659–60.
†*Pausanias: Description of Greece*, trans. W. H. S. Jones, 4:351.

remember all he has seen and heard, for Mnemosyne is "the holy wellspring" whose waters are for the "pure and healthy in hand and heart and who have no evil conscience in themselves."*

Long periods, perhaps lifetimes, are required before one is able fully to resist the seduction of Lethe. As aid thereto, the candidate invokes the fair goddess of Memory, not by empty ritual but with unshakable faith that Nous will at last stir Psyche to remembrance. Thomas Taylor (1758–1835), indefatigable translator of Greek and Neoplatonic classics, published in 1787 a small collection of Orphic Hymns, from which we reproduce the following:

To Mnemosyne, or the Goddess of Memory.

The consort I invoke of Jove divine,
Source of the holy, sweetly speaking Nine [Muses];
Free from th' oblivion of the fallen mind,
By whom the soul with intellect is join'd.
Reason's increase and thought to thee belong,
All-powerful, pleasant, vigilant, and strong.
'Tis thine to waken from lethargic rest
All thoughts deposited within the breast;
And nought neglecting, vig'rous to excite
The mental eye from dark oblivion's night.
*Come, blessed pow'r, thy mystics' mem'ry wake
To holy rites, and Lethe's fetters break.*†

**Inscriptiones Graecae Insularum Maris Aegaei* 1:789; quoted by Harold R. Willoughby, *Pagan Regeneration: A Study of Mystery Initiations in the Graeco-Roman World*, p. 44.

†Thomas Taylor, *The Mystical Hymns of Orpheus: Translated from the Greek, and demonstrated to be the Invocations which were used in the Eleusinian Mysteries*, p. 146.

It is remarkable that we have these testimonials of a wisdom that speak to the immortal and not merely to the ephemeral. The duty of Mnemosyne is plain: with vigor and exactitude to waken us to our true heritage so that consciously we will begin the ages-long task of loosening the bonds of self-centered and matter-based thinking. Then, prudently partaking of the spring of Forgetfulness, and drinking deep of the cooling waters from the Lake of Memory, we may rightfully utter the ancestral password:

I am a child of Earth and of Starry Heaven;
But my race is of Heaven (alone).

The descent into Hades completed, the successful candidate returns to light clothed with the radiance of things seen and remembered. That the independent experiences of each might be recorded while still fresh in memory, upon ascending from the grotto of Trophonius for example, the one newly-born was required "to dedicate a tablet on which is written all that each has heard or seen."* Thus Pausanias reports what he had learned from personal experience and also from others who had undergone the sacred rite.

So much for the daring disciple of ancient or modern Mysteries. But what about you and me, who may feel genuine nostalgia for knowledge of things unseen? Most of us still require the sweet oblivion of sleep and partial non-awareness until we have sufficiently grown in self-knowledge, judgment, and compassion. Imprisoned though we may be by self-made bonds, a part of us longs to awaken our "mystic memory" of holy things.

---

*Pausanias: Description of Greece 4:355.

Why don't we remember our past? Plato gives us a hint in Book 10 of his *Republic* (§§614–21), where he recounts the vision of Er. His was not so much a vision as a conscious following of the soul's experiences in the interim between lives. Er, son of Armenius, was thought to have been slain. He lay on the battlefield with other fallen heroes but, after ten days, when his body unlike the others showed no decay, it was taken home to be buried. Two days later Er wakened on a funeral pyre and shared his vision of the inner worlds, revealing that the character of the afterdeath journey among the planetary spheres is dependent upon the quality of a person's deeds while here on earth.

There were openings to the left leading below, he said, and openings to the right leading upwards. Those who had committed "unjust" deeds went down into the lower worlds, not to suffer torture forevermore, but long enough to learn their lessons. After they were purified, they went upwards midway to meet the souls of the "just" returning from the heavenly worlds where they had experienced things of great beauty. Er followed the passage of the souls through the planetary spheres and on their return to earth they came upon the Spinners of Destiny, the three Moirai or Fates: Lachesis, Clotho, and Atropos — Past, Present, and Future. They spin the fate of each individual soul as it passes through their realm. All chose lots (their future lives) according to their previous experiences. Finally, the souls came to the arid Plain of Forgetfulness (Lethe) where they were obliged to drink of its waters; but those not "saved by wisdom drank more than was necessary."

Does this not explain our condition here on earth?

Some of us drank perhaps too much of the waters of Forgetfulness, and therefore have had difficulty understanding what life is all about. Nonetheless, a part of us shunned the lethal waters, so that ancient memories still haunt us. Do we not feel at times the stirring of a forgotten wisdom? It is those memories, faint though they may be, that lead us into the very experiences in this life that will allow us to remember who we are and to become mindful of our heritage and our future destiny.

How does the forgetting of past lives relate to the popular practice of regressing a person, whether under hypnosis, drugs, or by other means, so that a person "relives" experiences he supposedly went through in childhood, in the prenatal stage or, as many believe, in a former life or lives? Dozens of books relating accounts of "previous lives" of those regressed have been published in recent decades.

This is not to deny the possibility that certain "memories" revealed under hypnotherapy may be true, in part at least, and could be helpful if interpreted correctly. If memory inheres in every portion of the physical brain, as some believe, it stands to reason that its cells, astral and/or physical, must bear within them the imprint of our long past, however deeply hidden. Memory is elusive. How many of us can recall in detail events of only a few years ago? Yet some seemingly chance incident, sound, or scent will suddenly release a flood of memories into our consciousness.

The native wisdom of many older peoples as well as theosophical teaching holds that our mind/soul has access to hidden reserves of memory from our ages-long past; further, and most significant, that a living, conscious entity oversees the growth of its future body. More permanent than the memory residing in our physical brain is that retained by the inner aspects of our being. While memory may reside in the life-atoms of the astral brain, the model of the physical brain, it adheres more permanently in the memory cells of character, in the reincarnating ego.

Ongoing research in prenatal and neonatal consciousness suggests that the fetal consciousness even during the first trimester records neural responses to what is pleasing to it and what is not, and also reacts instantaneously to what it hears as well as to the unspoken thoughts and feelings of *both* parents. As a living entity, though not yet housed in a body like ours, whatever the fetus experiences is registered in the astral light as well as in its memory cells. The newborn has no apparent recollection of this, but studies confirm that the level of awareness of the returning ego is far more acute than previously suspected.*

The mystery of memory is indeed profound, and we know very little about its role during life and after death. Even without regression, it is possible for an individual when fully awake to "see" into the astral atmosphere of earth, the astral light, and momentarily "relive" or "remember" persons or events that may or may not derive from his own karmic past. As with regression, it is equally possible for one to be "seeing" or "reading" in the astral light the thoughts or life-experiences of someone else. When so little firm knowledge is available in this field, it is well to be prudent and not make hard-and-fast judgments. The pro-

---

*See Thomas Verny, M.D., with John Kelly, *The Secret Life of the Unborn Child.*

cess of regression with or without hypnosis neither proves nor disproves reincarnation.

It is regrettable that the popularization of regression practices has given a confused picture of the doctrine of reincarnation, due in the main to the overemphasis placed on the role of the persona, the mask worn by the reimbodying human monad as it incarnates in life after life on earth. It is natural to want to know who we were in our last life, but such knowledge is double-edged. To undergo hypnotic regression simply to satisfy the hunger of people to know who they were in a previous life is morally and psychically questionable. Sufficient unto this life are the challenges thereof.

We can be certain that — whether in the astral life-atoms of our brain or in the higher elements of our constitution, as well as in the astral light of earth — all that we *are*, since we first became thinking, self-choosing humans, has been and is recorded. This ties in with Plato's views that the soul has a memory of its own. In his Dialogues, particularly in *Meno* (§81b), he speaks of the process of re-collection or remembering — not memorizing in the sense of learning by rote but of reminiscing, re-bringing forth memory of the wisdom the soul had anciently attained. The soul, he affirmed, has a reservoir of experience from the past and "if one is strenuous and does not faint" in his endeavor to recall, to re-collect this wisdom, suddenly, as in a flash, there may come a revelation, a light streaming into the consciousness from within.

7

Karma

MUCH THOUGHT IS BEING GIVEN these days to our brotherhood with the whole of nature, that we are linked with sun, moon, and stars as closely as we are with the kingdoms coming after us. Here is oneness of essence of every god-spark throughout space because of identity of source in the Unfathomable; and yet, since each bears the fruitage of aeons of evolving, every god-spark is impressed with its unique seal of divinity. A oneness, but with differences — and herein lies the secret of life's unending mystery. This suggests that a vast treasury of individual karmic experience is capsuled within the core of each of us. In brief, we are one with all others in our inmost self, yet every human being has his essential quality or character, his distinctive grain, as it were, running true to form throughout his nature.

Stoic philosophers of ancient Greece and Rome understood that within the cosmos, as well as within every one of its myriad lives, was a creative power which held the plan or purpose, the "reason" for its being, which they named *logos*. To them logos is *spermatikos*, "seed-bearing," and from it a host of individual "seed-logoi" come into manifested existence, eventually to return to their source: "indestructible seed-powers, countless in number . . . spread throughout the universe, everywhere shaping, peopling, designing, multiplying . . ."*

Throughout its earth cycle, each of these myriad seed-logoi is evolving and therefore making karma, and in so doing is affecting other seed-logoi which in turn affect the destiny of each. It is this interrelationship and intermingling of karmas that make our lives difficult to understand at times. Problems arise now and then because we tend to think of karma as something inflicted upon us by an outside force, a kind of nemesis or dread fate falling upon us when we are least prepared, avenging some unknown deeds done, or left undone, in this life or in lives long past. In reality karma is an outflowing of our very self. Seldom do we look upon the universal law of cause and effect as healing, merciful because of its restorative power.

With the earliest Greeks, Nemesis was a goddess who personified our conscience, our inborn fear of committing wrong against the gods; also, our reverence for the moral and spiritual law of harmony, of balance. We have forgotten that the gods are not separate from ourselves and that we are an extension of their life essence, their care for us being as intrinsic a part of our growing process as our protection is for the atomic lives evolving within the human hierarchy.

Naturally we ask ourselves what good it does to suffer the consequences in *this* life of deeds we don't remember committing in a previous life. We feel it would be fairer if we did remember, for if we knew where we had gone astray we would not object to meeting the consequences now; also,

---

*Edward Vernon Arnold, *Roman Stoicism*, p. 161.

we could more easily see where to make amends. Yet, when all is said and done, we *do* remember our past, for the past is ourselves: we are the karma, the fruit, of our ages-long experience unfolding itself in the present. True, our physical brain, being newly formed for this life, has little power of recall, but this is not all we are. The personalities we assume from life to life are strung on a "thread-self" (sūtrātman) like beads on a cord. While the beads or personalities are only partially conscious of the radiant self linking them together and from which they draw their life-force, our ātmic self or sūtrātman *does* remember. Something of the aroma of awareness carried over into each new personality may be intuited in moments of inner quiet.

Buddhist texts remind us that the time will come when we shall be required to gain knowledge, not only of our immediately preceding life, but of "the sequence of births and deaths."* By then we will have become sufficiently mature spiritually to handle such knowledge without injury to others or to ourselves, and will have earned the boon of instantaneous recall of the wisdom that is innately ours.

All of this leads to large reflections, taking us beyond the immediacy of present circumstances to previous incarnations, possibly even to former world cycles. We cannot envision a beginning beyond which no causes were set in motion, for every god-spark is a consciousness, a living being that has been pursuing its individual course of evolution for aeons. We humans, within the tidal flux and ebb of our

---

**Visuddhi Magga*, Buddhaghosa (5th c. AD); cf. *World of the Buddha*, ed. Lucien Stryk, p. 159 et seq.

planet's growth pattern, have likewise a long history of births and deaths, successes and failures; more important, our entry into earth life, whatever the situation or place, is an outflowing of our karma, the inevitable consequence of causes sown in former incarnations.

By the law of magnetic attraction, whatever comes to us we ourselves must at some time have set in motion, knowingly or not. Every instant of our lives we are impressing on our entire being the quality of our thinking and feeling, lofty or base. It is *we* who leave these imprints on our life-atoms and, as the soul returns again and again to earth, those very life-atoms also return to us, to form anew our several sheaths, physical, mental, and spiritual. No one reaps a harvest that is not of his or her own making — in benefits and strength of character for good seed sown; in deprivations and weakness of will for tares. Not only is karma the stern yet always beneficent recorder of every movement of consciousness for humans, but likewise for all entities from atomic to macrocosmic. To regard karma as an avenging demon or a rewarding angel is to judge by externals. Whatever its evolutionary standing, each entity is its own *lipika* or "scribe," its own recorder, awakener, and friend. Just as we leave our characteristic mark on every particle of our composite constitution, just so every other entity is doing likewise.

All of us undergo trials that are hard to justify from the narrow limits of a single life; we are subject to laws and influences that seemingly have little relation to our personal lives: national, racial, global, even solar and cosmic in scope. When kindly and thoughtful persons suffer a cruel fate it is incomprehensible that they could have committed terrible wrong in the past. And what about the inexpressible suffering of the many millions through famine, war, or natural catastrophe?

If, indeed, the one inviolable law in the universe is karma, whose face is compassion and whose reverse is justice, then in the final reckoning it is impossible for an individual to undergo any experience that ultimately does not derive from some portion of his constitution, which extends from the divine to the physical. As the workings of karma are mysterious, they are not easily discerned. What happens to one may not be the result of evil deeds in the past, but may well be impulsed by the higher self for its own benefic purposes. *Man's Search for Meaning* by the Austrian psychiatrist Viktor Frankl is moving testimony to the fact that out of the hell and horror of concentration camps heroes were born. The ordeal for each of them must have been an initiation of a most powerful sort.

The fact that a few tragically misguided people can plunge a whole nation of fine men and women into conditions that normally no one of them would tolerate, must have its seeding long ago. Ever since we were lighted with the fire of mind and became aware of ourselves as thinking beings, we have had the power to choose between right and wrong. For millions of years we have been responsible for our thoughts and emotions and the deeds that spring from them. Because of the power of choice, and because we are as yet imperfectly developed, we are bound to make wrong choices, especially when the pull of the material seems stronger than the pull of the spiritual.

Human nature evolves slowly and today, as in the past, we have a choice between selfish and unselfish instincts; between acting for our own benefit, or for the benefit of our family and community. With every decision we are setting in motion causes for good or ill, which eventually will have their effects upon us and our surroundings. To be able to trace the interwebbings of karma among nations would require a knowledge far beyond present human capability — a comprehension of the vast panorama of past sowing by nations and individuals long ages ago. As we each have our individual karma, and are born in a certain country at a certain time, we also to some degree participate in its national karma.

If we conceive that justice and harmony are inherent in the universal order and that nature ever works to restore disturbed equilibrium, we must conclude that everyone, barring none, is reaping the quality of experience that belongs to him. When we are beset with trials beyond our control, perhaps our higher self is rejoicing at the opportunity offered us to learn valued lessons, nurture compassion and, possibly, in these particular circumstances to be of quiet help to those around us in greater need than we. Have we not all discovered, usually after many years, that the harshest passages of our life yielded lasting gifts? "Blessings in disguise" is the common phrase, suggesting an intuitive recognition that pain and sorrow hold hidden beauties, not least in our deepened love and understanding for those in travail.

Having suffered the illness and death of many close friends, I have thought often, "If only I had the power to heal; if only I could bring surcease of pain." As I have grown older I have come to realize that this may not be the wisest and most compassionate way to help. I have come to understand that the kindest and most effective way to sustain another is to help him find the courage and the love and the confidence to meet his karma creatively. Of course we should use the medical aids that are normally available, but let us allow our friend the honor and the dignity of recognizing that he has the capacity to handle his karma with understanding. Maybe his body will die earlier than the norm, but in meeting the karma that is his, he is accepting consciously the privilege of working through a heavy karmic experience for a beneficent purpose. There is solace and strength for both the dying and the living in being able to take this attitude.

How best can we stand by? By getting down and weeping with our friend? Yes, there may be tears, tears of understanding and love, not of pity and despondency; tears of recognition that the soul has the courage to take on a severe ordeal, knowing that a great cleansing process is going on, a clearing of the karma for the future. It doesn't need a lot of words — words are often quite unnecessary. But there has to be a willingness to be strong, steadfast, and loyal, so that our friend may draw on our caring strength when he most needs it.

How do we know what the soul must undergo to be truly free? How do we know that the terrible suffering, which may in a sense be worse for the bystander than for the one going through it, is not the very karma that the soul has been yearning for? But to shrug off another's pain is diabolic and leads to hardness of heart. Such an attitude is to miss the whole purpose of life. We must relieve suffering as far as we can; in every possible way we must share our sympathy and understanding — not by lifting the burden from another's shoulders, but by helping him to meet and carry his life's challenges with greater confidence in himself and in the larger perspective.

When we reflect on the meaning of disabling affliction, be it physical, psychological, or mental — often calling for infinite resources of patience and love — we are bound to ask *why*? Why are some born into a tortured body, or others struck down by crippling accident or illness? What assigns one to a life of advantage, while another, possibly with richer potential, has to fight every inch of the way just to handle a body nonresponsive to normal command, and then is obliged often to work far more intensively to achieve a flowering of mind and spirit? Millions of people today are carrying a burden of private sorrow and asking themselves where is the justice and mercy in a universe supposedly administered by an all-loving God? It is cold comfort indeed to anguished parents to be told it is God's will, the decree of Allah, or the working out of old karma.

The cause and cure of suffering reach to the core of mystery and will remain beyond our comprehension, beyond the words of all the teachings humanity has received, until we can *feel* with every atom of our being the compassion of divine purpose behind all that happens. Certainly no one can say categorically that a child born with a congenital malformation is paying for some misdeed in a previous life or lives. It may well be the case; but equally it may not be so at all. Is it not conceivable, for example, that a returning entity — for we are primarily spirit-souls, not bodies — could be far enough advanced interiorly to "choose" the karma of severe deprivation in order to gain a profound empathy with all who suffer? Is it not also possible that a reincarnating ego, in need of temporary respite from certain mental and emotional pressures, selects a "retarded" vehicle for an incarnation? Again, it could be that cruelty or selfishness had been so ingrained in the character that the surest means of removing the warp is to take birth in an impaired body so that empathy and compassion might be burned deep into the soul and the nature gentled.

"Judge not that ye be not judged" — only one able to read the spiritual history of an individual would be able to determine just what lines of karma had been traced in lives long gone that culminated in the precise conditions which the reincarnating ego now finds itself handling — or not handling — in this life. All of us have been weaving grandeur and baseness into the tapestry of our soul; but when we intuit, as many do, that we are linked with our divine parent and that whatever we experience of joy or pain is an intrinsic part of our destiny that we have been building for cycles beyond number, we *know* that there is a fitness and a beauty in even the most heartrending of circumstances.

A letter typewritten with a mouth-stick by a friend, who from birth has weathered the trauma of severe disablement, bears this out. Viola Henne earns her living as an artist, and devotes what time and energy she can to working with children and young adults who are more incapacitated than she is. Viola is not concerned with what they can't do; she focuses on what they *can* do. In this way she energizes their will and creative talent to bring forth whatever potential they have. She writes:

> Please promote erasing the false idea that people get about the word "karma." Neither I nor others handicapped have been "punished" by being *in* damaged bodies (brains, or . . .). No! In fact, once one's consciousness has sprung past the illusions of faulty education, then in a flash one changes one's attitude about the disability — changes and realizes once and forever that the damaged form is not a punishment but a holy privilege, through which one is at last permitted to "work" on a conscious (awakened) level.
>
> It's like wearing a proper costume to "go to work" — the damaged vehicle is a necessary and self-imposed outer draping. Our own inner mechanisms permit the current "body" and momentary circumstances so that the teaching-learning conditions may be met. Each of us has in some moment of time had to "pay" for past errors in thought or deed. Able-bodied people are not purer than cripples; they "pay" for their errors via a different cause-and-effect situation.
>
> Karma — the word should be explained as meaning "circumstances currently the soul chose as the best opportunity for the soul's growth and for teaching others."

A powerful response to the question "Is life fair?" by one who refused to stay bitter and has consecrated her gift of courage and love to all in need of hope and self-worth. Even when someone's life is heavy with trial, to feel that he or she has a very "bad" karma this time round is to hold a totally mistaken view from the standpoint of the human soul or reincarnating ego. Purucker said it well: "we are our own karma," meaning by this that everything that comes to us, in character or in circumstance, is an outflowing of ourselves — our past. If we or those we love have trying and painful circumstances to go through, ill health, personal reverses, or the like, this is not "bad" karma. Admittedly, it may be an extremely difficult karma to meet, but if in the long run it furthers the progress of the soul, it must be counted beneficent.

This is one of the most helpful ideas because many today are feeling crushed under the weight of life's burdens. When we realize that *we* are our karma, then we know that whatever is unrolling before us is really ourselves having the opportunity to learn and to grow and to deepen our perceptions and our understanding. As our sympathies expand beyond the periphery of our personal problems and we observe the humor and dignity with which others, seemingly less favored than ourselves, face their life situation, we may discover that those of us who have the most difficulty in handling our character failings are the more disadvantaged. A bit of self-examination is therapeutic, reminding us that we are all fellow climbers, and that those who appear to be making little progress may well be clearing the way of obstacles for themselves and for others behind them that otherwise might have proved insurmountable.

Of course, it is easy to philosophize when one has reasonably sound health and comfortable circumstances. But what of the poverty-stricken, and those doomed to die of disease or starvation? Shall we say it is their karma and they will have to work through it, with better luck, hopefully, next life? Such an attitude would be reprehensible. Obviously, it is their karma or they wouldn't have to meet those conditions; but how can we isolate their karma from our own? We are *one* family, and all of us have had a share in creating the present difficult circumstances. Besides, is it not also *our* karma to be profoundly concerned, and if at all possible to help alleviate the awful misery that exists in so many parts of our globe? There is some consolation in the fact that the world conscience is awakening and becoming more sensitive and acute, so that an increasing number of self-sacrificing and knowledgeable men and women are already dedicating their lives to practical humanitarian service.

Much as our hearts yearn to be of help, many of us can offer little in the way of tangible relief. But there is not one of us who cannot work to eradicate the *causes* — deep-seated and long in the making — that have resulted in humanity's plight. This is an enormously long-range goal, admittedly, but does this make it any the less worthy? In a letter written in 1889 to the American theosophists assembled in convention, HPB quotes these lines from one of her teachers:

> "Let not the fruit of good Karma be your motive; for your Karma, good or bad, being one and the common property of all mankind, nothing good or bad can happen to you that is not shared by many others." . . . "There is no happiness for one who is ever thinking of Self and forgetting all other Selves."

And then this telling sentence:

> "The Universe groans under the weight of such action

(Karma), and none other than self-sacrificial Karma relieves it."*

This is provocative, and is there one human being to whom it does not apply? Indeed, the universe groans under the weight of our selfish acts and thoughts, and it is we, individually and collectively, who are responsible insofar as we contribute to that weight. Being human, all of us have mixed motives to a degree; but we have before us the grand ideal of making our lives altruistic. This is a goal that requires many lifetimes to attain, but it is a goal worth keeping ever living in our hearts. When it becomes the dominant influence in our daily experience, we shall express a larger measure of unselfishness than of its opposite.

Selfishness inhibits the natural growth of the soul; it is inimical to the growth of mankind, because it is a turning in upon oneself. Conversely, not thinking ourselves to be of first importance releases light from within, and the light which flows into our souls bursts the barriers of our personalities and sheds a radiance upon the lives of others. It is a fact that every altruistic impulse and aspiration, uniting with an elemental being, sends its influence into the thought atmosphere of our world, and every individual who is in sympathetic vibration with that quality of aspiration responds in kind. His life is ennobled and his surroundings irradiated. In like manner the opposite is true, and for this also we are accountable.

No matter what outer circumstances karma may place us in, we can always remember that we are souls, each of us having his individual dharma to fulfill. Krishna tells Arjuna

---

*H. P. Blavatsky to the American Conventions: 1888–1891, p. 22.

that the dharma of another is full of peril, and even if it is not the most excellent path, he is admonished to fulfill the dharma that belongs to the self (*sva-dharma*).* In this way he shall be following his own path, and doing that for which he was born into this world.

Orientalists have translated dharma variously — duty, truth, law, religion, piety — but all those words are only an approach, they do not convey the richness of thought imbodied in the Sanskrit term. Dharma, from the verb *dhṛi*, "to bear, to carry, to sustain," implies that each of us came into incarnation bearing a destiny that is ours, sustaining the truth of our inner being as we fulfill our outward duties to the best of our ability. We have first to recognize our destiny as being within, not outside of ourselves. We don't have to go to Tibet, America, Thailand, or Africa to find it. *We* are our destiny, our karma, our individual dharma.

There is so much awry in human relationships all over the world that it may take many ages to set things right; no doubt we've tallied up quite a karmic score against us that must be balanced. But we should not overlook the other side of the ledger, the nobler entries made in this life and in lives gone by. Could it not be that the intensity of global and individual suffering and confusion of values is due as much to a karmic awakening, a stimulus from our higher selves, as it is to karmic debts still unpaid?

Surely we were meant to live our lives as a wholeness and not be continually fractured by anguish or despair. Sorrow

---

**Bhagavad-Gītā* 3:35 (W. Q. Judge recension, p. 21).

comes to us all, but like rain to Mother Earth it should nourish and bring new growth. So let us give ample room for joy in our lives, the inner joy that warms the heart and balances the karmic scales. One day, in this life or in another, we may be able to look at all we have been through with the eyes of the seer we intrinsically are — as an eagle high above our earth karma — and glimpse with panoramic vision our entire experience, past and present, in terms of motivation as well as in deeds. We shall *know* that all hindrances, all suffering, physical and mental, and also death, are part of the natural pattern of growth, etching into the soul the larger perception, the truer love, the deeper caring for all.

8

Karma and/or Grace

THE DOGMA THAT A SAVIOR "died for our sins" has been much misunderstood, for there is great beauty in the doctrine of the incarnation of a divinity in human form: "For God so loved the world, that he gave his only begotten Son" (*John* 3:16). This is the Christian way of saying that the gods took pity on humankind and sent a ray of themselves into the soul of a noble human being so that in his work among mankind he could more potently manifest the light of divinity — not so that he might save us from our sins or wash away the karma of our transgression against ourselves and others. What we have done, we are responsible for. What we think, we must atone for or receive benefit from. There is no absolution except by ourselves. Paul's statement on the universally applicable law of cause and effect, kismet or karma, is refreshingly straight to the point:

> If the Spirit is the source of our life, let the Spirit also direct our course. . . .
> Make no mistake about this: God is not to be fooled; a man reaps what he sows. If he sows seed in the field of his lower nature, he will reap from it a harvest of corruption, but if he sows in the field of the Spirit, the Spirit will bring him a harvest of eternal life. So let us never tire of doing good, for if we do not slacken our efforts we shall in due time reap our

harvest. Therefore, as opportunity offers, let us work for the good of all . . .
— *Galatians* 5:25; 6:7–10 (*The New English Bible*)

In short, every moment of every day we are setting new causes in motion and reaping effects of past deeds. It is the quality of our motive that has shaped and will continue to shape our character and our future. Because we are one humanity and not separate, we are affecting the destiny not only of those with whom we associate, but also of thousands of others sensitive to our wavelength. If we are altruistically motivated, we shall be sowing in the realms of the spirit; if self-serving, our sowing will be in the field of our personal self. We reap as we sow, for nature reacts impersonally without reference to pleasing or displeasing the sower. The harvest will conform to the sowing since every human being is his own reaper and recorder, impressing what he *is* on the memory cells of character and, in fact, on every level of his being.

How does this jibe with the idea of grace? As used in the New Testament, grace signifies almost exclusively God's means of granting forgiveness for sin through the intermediary of Christ Jesus. "He that believeth . . . shall be saved" (*Mark* 16:16). Whatever an individual may have been or done, by accepting Christ as his Savior he is assured freedom from guilt and the blessing of God's grace. Read literally, as it is by the more orthodox Christian, it is unconscionable: what kind of justice is this if a reprobate can, simply through accepting Jesus as the only son of God, have his record wiped clean and his character purged of iniquity? Is there no requisite of atonement for wrongdoing? And what about the injury done to others through one's brutal and thoughtless acts? From the standpoint of human, let alone divine justice, it is unthinkable to countenance the remission of sins through God's forgiveness, and this only for believers to boot; it is opposed to all that humanity deems ethical and fair. Interpreted, however, within the context of Jesus' injunction, "go, and sin no more," the verse from Mark becomes profoundly significant, the more so when linked with Jesus' statement to Nicodemus that "Except a man be born again, he cannot see the kingdom of God."

> Except a man be born of water, and of the Spirit, he cannot enter into the kingdom of God. That which is born of the flesh, is flesh; and that which is born of the Spirit, is spirit. Marvel not that I said unto thee, Ye must be born again. — *John* 3:3, 5–7 (Authorized Version)

The story of Saul of Tarsus is an example in point. Reared in the traditions of his people, he found the burden of guilt for past sin becoming intolerable, so much so that he could not identify with his God. As a Hebrew he knew he must earn God's acceptance through moral rectitude and the fulfillment of his commandments. So distraught was he that he took out his anger and despair on those who followed this stranger, Jesus. Then one day while en route to Damascus a light suddenly enveloped Saul, shining with such intensity that he fell down blinded, and he heard the Lord calling to him. After three days he was "a new creature," his sight was restored, the past gone, even in time his name. Had his strong yearning to find meaning in life momentarily opened his soul to his own inner light?

Now, as Paul, he entered upon his new life charged with extraordinary vigor, exhorting all to whom he spoke and wrote to follow the way of the spirit rather than that of the flesh: "Therefore, if any man be in Christ, he is a new creature: old things are passed away; behold, all things are become new" (*2 Corinthians* 5:17). Where there is true conversion, a "turning" from the obstructionist ways of the past and a total immersion of the soul in the life of the spirit, he is as one "new born" — not because his past karma is erased but because he himself is inwardly renewed, "born of the Spirit." Henceforth he approaches life with a new vision and a strengthened will.

It is a beautiful truth anciently known that for every utterly sincere move made in the direction of one's inner divinity, it responds in kind and a radiance shines upon the heart and mind of the aspirant. Without question, sustained effort to renovate the life through earnest aspiration and cultivation of the will for unselfish goals allows a "clearing" to occur and the voice of intuition to make itself heard. Whether this be the voice of the Lord or other deity, or that of one's inner god, is immaterial. "Go, and sin no more" has many applications, but woe to the individual who does not try to live up to the obligation assumed: to merit the grace of divine acceptance.

Most important, an act of grace, whatever its source and however experienced, *by no means implies an abrogation of the law of karma*, or that the follies and errors of former days are erased from our individual Book of Destiny. Whatever we have done or omitted to do before our transformation must be resolved, in this or in future lives — and this ought to be happily met, for affliction is a welcomed opportunity to clear the slate and set to right ancient wrongs. Equally significant, all that we have longed to do and to be, all the silent, unrecognized yearnings to be a light in the darkness of our environs, are faithfully entered on the imperishable records of eternity, to return in due season as blessings, a gift of grace for ourselves and others, flowing forth in strict harmony with karmic law.

We can view the dogma of Jesus' "dying for our sins" from another perspective. The fact that great teachers are sent forth at cyclic periods to work among this or that people suggests that they come for a sacred purpose: to stimulate aspiration in the souls of all who will heed the call. The appearance of such an incarnation of a divine radiance marks the descent of a divine energy on earth which coincides with the upsurging call from human hearts. The intersection of human and divine cycles thus has a twofold purpose. As the spirit-soul of the chosen vessel fuses with divinity there occurs an explosion of such tremendous potency that the lightning of the gods bursts upon mankind, to energize our thought-world with divine-spiritual magnetism. It has happened in the past; it will happen again when we call it forth.

There is a linkage of karmas all along the way, a linkage between the god-worlds and ourselves. Tradition has it that divine beings or avatāras enter earth as a kind of underworld, and thus "die" to their own high realms, and by so doing undergo an initiation — a majestic thought. In deliberately taking birth among earthlings, a part of them dies — there is a "dying for our sins," literally and metaphorically. Like a stream of light and compassion across human destinies, they leave their impress. By virtue of their having left a portion of their divine energy in the world, in a certain mystical sense they take on part of humanity's karma. While it is we who must liberate ourselves, everybody who turns toward the light within and is touched thereby — be it ever so slightly — to that degree links his karma with that of the Great Ones.

If, then, we are responsible for "saving" ourselves, God does not predestine human beings to a life of either eternal heaven or eternal damnation. Yet we cannot leave it at that, for there is a grain of truth in the concept of predestination, in that *we* have predestined ourselves from the past to be what we are now. This implies that certain karmic lines of events and of character are foreordained — not by some god or being external to us, but *by ourselves*. As Shakespeare says: "There's a divinity that shapes our ends, Rough-hew them how we will."* That divinity is our own deepest self; *we* are the ones who shape our destiny with our free will. How we meet the events and circumstances of life, and the relationships among our fellow humans, is in our hands every moment. In the process we are shaping and reshaping our character and future destiny. Nothing can happen outside of the laws of karma; and as each of us *is* our karma, we are the fruitage, the result, the expression of our entire past. Each of us therefore is the recorder of our own karmic destiny.

The Passion of Christ represents a profoundly sacred

**Hamlet*, Act V, scene ii.

experience undergone by every savior willingly, as an act of pure compassion, that the ideal of spiritual conquest might be firmly enshrined in the consciousness of man. The Gospel narrative is a story of the human soul, and Jesus represents the divine climax of what every person on earth may one day achieve — the bringing to birth of the Christ-sun within his own heart. This does not imply a promise of victory without merit; each must achieve self-mastery by individual effort. Though we may be spirits in chains, we are spirits, not chains, and no power on earth or in heaven can imprison forever the human spirit. While history chronicles the tragedy of human failure, a higher history testifies to the unconquered human spirit, for the passion and triumph of a Christos delineates the sunward path that every human being must eventually choose.

9

The Christian Message

I

TRUTH IS FOUND IN ALL SACRED writings if we dig deep enough beneath dogma and ritual to find the rich ore of esotericism. The Judeo-Christian genesis story was never intended to be taken literally, any more than were the creation myths of Tahiti or ancient Persia, China or the Americas. The oral and written traditions of every people, in varying metaphor and symbol, point to the awesome moment in beginningless time when Darkness became Light and from the deeps of Silence came the sounding of Logos, the Word, causing gods and stars to sing together for the sheer joy of being and becoming.

How "nothingness" is able to bring forth a universe with its hosts of lives of every type and grade is a perennial mystery. How does zero become one and one beget two, then three, to produce in turn myriads of living beings, from stars to humans, animals to atoms? When all is formless and void, who or what initiates the first quiver of rhythmic pulsation within the vast expanses of Chaos?

Those versed in the ancient Jewish theosophy of Qabbālāh repeatedly cite certain passages from the *Zohar* — the best known Qabbalistic treatise constituting a running commentary on the Tōrāh, the sacred "Law" of the Hebrews — which affirm that he who would penetrate to the kernel of meaning hidden within the Tōrāh must peel off husk after husk to reach the soul. If he would intuit essence, he must peel off still further layers, for within every word and sentence is a high mystery. "But the wise, whose wisdom makes them full of eyes, pierce through the garment to the very essence of the word that is hidden thereby."*

Paradoxically, while to us the universe *in essence* is uncreate and infinite, without beginning and without end, every *manifested* universe has a point of origin, a coming forth out of "nothingness," out of Darkness into Light, and the succession of lives that ensue. The Qabbālāh envisions three stages of non-existence between the Darkness of the Deep of *Genesis* and the coming forth of Light: 1) *'ayin*, "nothing," nonbeing, the void, beyond all power of conception; 2) *'ēin sōf*, "no limit, without end," the limitless or endless expanse; and 3) *'ēin sōf ōr*, "no limit light," boundless light.

When *'ēin sōf*, impelled by divine thought and will and the mysterious power of contraction and expansion, wished to manifest a portion of itself, it concentrated its essence into a single point. This the Qabbalists called *Keter* (Kether), "Crown," the first emanation of Light, and from this primordial point burst forth "nine splendid lights."

In an attempt to clarify what will always remain an "impenetrable mystery," the Qabbalists imaged the wondrous process of the One becoming the many in varying ways,

---

**The Zohar (iii:98b), trans. Harry Sperling, Maurice Simon, and Dr. Paul P. Levertoff, 3:300.

most often as a Tree of Life composed of ten *Sefīrōt*, ten "numbers" or emanations from 'ēin sōf, the boundless, making a tenfold universe. "Amid the insupportable brilliance" of 'ēin sōf 'ōr, boundless light, they visualized the head of *Ādām Qadmōn,* Ideal or Archetypal Man, the first of four Adams which manifest in four Worlds of descending spiritual stature. The fourth Adam on the fourth world, our earth, ushers in and becomes our present humanity. In other words, on each of the four worlds a tenfold Tree of Life, manifesting along with Archetypal Man, clothes itself in ever more material forms. At length, the fourth world, is able to sustain the mineral, vegetable, and animal kingdoms; and on this world humanity, from being originally asexual, then androgynous, now functions as man and woman.*

In this manner the *Zohar* interprets the first few verses of *Genesis,* commencing with God (really "gods," 'elohīm), forming from themselves the heavens (also plural in the Hebrew) and the earth, which was formless and void until the quickening when the Spirit of God (*rūaḥ 'elohīm,* "breath of the 'elohīm") fecundated the waters of space.

During the last 2,000 years the word *god* has come to have a very narrow and fixed meaning in contradistinction to the broad and fluidic connotation it enjoyed all through the Graeco-Roman world and the Near East. At that time the relationship between gods and humans was intimate,

---

*The reader is referred to the following sources: *Major Trends in Jewish Mysticism* by Gershom G. Scholem, notably the chapter titled: "The Zohar II: The Theosophic Doctrine of the Zohar," p. 202 ff.; *The Zohar,* translated by Harry Sperling and Maurice Simon, 5 vols.; *Qabbalah* by Isaac Myer; *Kabbalah: New Perspectives* by Moshe Idel.

gods at times taking human form, and worthy humans attaining the status of godhood. Due to centuries of imposed theological dicta, the word God today generally connotes the Supreme Being or Creator who created the heaven and the earth, and all creatures thereon, i.e., extracosmic, distinct and apart from his creation. Without question, a great many Christians, barring the most rigid of fundamentalist sects, have abandoned the notion of a personal God in the likeness of a man with a long beard, sitting on a throne among the clouds and handing out rewards and punishments according to whim or caprice.

Assuredly, every human being is a spark of that divine Intelligence, with his own inner god at the core of his being. Could any entity, even a dust mote, exist were it not the outermost expression of its unique god-essence? Indeed, every atomic particle is a god-spark imbodying itself in material form. As such it is one in essence with the divinity at the heart of Being. This means that the monads or inner gods at the heart of each of the trillions upon trillions of atoms in all of nature's kingdoms and throughout the cosmos are likewise *one in essence* — truly a universal kinship of spirit. When we image God as infinite, our perception of the Divine Will becomes as unrestricted as thought and aspiration allow. Is God transcendent or immanent, outside of us or within? The question is redundant if divinity permeates all. Under the press of daily concerns, we tend to forget who we are and the destiny that is ahead not only for us humans but for every monadic life, be it an atom in the brain of an earthworm or in one of Saturn's rings.

In the *Gospel according to John* (10:34), Jesus reminded

those who reviled him: "Is it not written in your law, I said, Ye are gods?" — a theme Paul enlarged upon in writing to the people of Corinth: "what communion hath light with darkness? . . . ye are the temple of the living God" (*2 Cor.* 6:14, 16) and "the Spirit of God dwelleth in you" (*1 Cor.* 3:16). In view of these verses, often quoted from pulpit and in literature, how is it that for centuries we have erroneously been taught we were "born in sin"?

The allegory of Adam and Eve's fall from grace and their dismissal from the Garden of Eden, instead of representing a transgression, has an exhilarating effect when interpreted as the awakening of mind in early humanity. In order for the early humans (ourselves) to become as gods, we had to "die" from our Eden state of unconscious bliss and take on the challenge of self-awareness of our divine potential. In the process we were obliged to put on "coats of skin" as we imbodied in worlds of matter. Now we are earning our way out of the "sin" of our material condition by the sweat of our brow, spiritually and intellectually, and eventually we shall assume the dignity of our heritage and become fully evolved divinities.

What, then, of Jesus and the story of his life as told in the New Testament? Many Christians no longer regard the Gospel narratives as factual accounts of a historic figure. Some prefer to read in them a symbolic record of the initiatory experience of a savior — of every savior who comes according to cyclic need. Some deny any *special* divinity to Jesus, seeing him rather as a noble exemplar of humanhood, worthy of emulation. Others, possibly millions, devoutly hold Jesus to be the *only* Son of God and that solely through believing in him can they be saved. Three conclusions, apparently incompatible; yet when we view them as three ways of looking at Jesus, we get a fairly rounded picture of what he represents.

Simply put, the idea that Jesus came to be a light to the world and to "save us from our sins" shows us how *we* could save ourselves, how we could free ourselves from bondage and from the tomb of material things — not that we could do whatever we like and then just before we die repent, shift the burden of our guilt on him, and be saved forever and forever.

Gautama Buddha, too, was a light to the world. In fact, when we compare the well-known incidents in the lives of Gautama and Jesus we find an astonishing correspondence: both were born of a virgin mother; both were schooled in and drew inspiration from the sacred traditions of their respective homelands, and rebelled against the orthodoxy of their respective priesthoods; both cut through all barriers of class and religious bias and accepted as disciples whoever was earnest of heart. Emphasis on the "light" within by both Jesus and Gautama assured a divine equality of opportunity to every human being: to Brahman and outcaste, Sadducee and leper, king, courtesan, and fisherman. Notably, Jesus' transfiguration when "his face did shine as the sun, and his raiment was white as the light" is reminiscent of Gautama's enlightenment and his attainment of final nirvana when the color of the Tathāgata's skin became so "clear and exceeding bright" that his robes of cloth of gold lost their splendor.* Last but far from least, their coming to

---

*Matthew 17:2; *Mahā-Parinibbāna-Sutta,* iv, §§48–50.

earth because of an immense love for mankind — sent by God as a divine Incarnation in the case of Jesus; in consequence of a vow registered lives ago in the case of Gautama — marks them as links in the chain of compassionate Guardians who watch over and inspire us to follow the inward way.*

Inevitably, the colorful accounts of their birth, ministry, and death are in large part allegory. Whatever there be of solid history in the canonical Gospels or in Buddhist scriptures of both Northern and Southern Schools is clothed in metaphor and legend, so that it is difficult to separate fact from fantasy. Nonetheless, the similarities are too close to ignore, and cause one to question whether the chroniclers may have patterned their respective narratives on some ancient sacred prototype.

In all probability they did, for striking parallels are to be found in the life stories of a number of other world saviors. Persians of old tell of the trials and conquests of Mithras and of a series of Zoroasters; in Mexico Quetzalcoatl, the feathered serpent, was "crucified" and rose from the dead; similarly, the sun gods of the Phrygians and other peoples of Asia Minor suffered death and abuse, as did the Norse Odin

---

*One may speculate just how potent an influence was exerted by Asian pilgrims on the Judean Gospel writers. Aside from commercial traffic between the Indian subcontinent and the Hellenic world subsequent to the conquests of Alexander in the 4th century BC, for approximately 700 years thereafter the Library and Museum at Alexandria were centers of spiritual and intellectual intercourse among Buddhists, Persians, Arabs, Hebrews, Greeks, Romans, and of course Egyptians and other peoples surrounding the Mediterranean Basin; probably also Hindus and Chinese.

who hung nine nights, spear-pierced, on the "windtorn tree" of life.* Is it then so extraordinary that Jesus who became Christos (Anointed, Messiah) should also have experienced a like travail and glorification?

II

The drama of Jesus begins with the story of his strange and beautiful birth at the winter solstice of a virgin mother, with a star guiding wise men from the East. Similar virgin births are recorded of other Savior figures, such as of the legendary Persian teacher Mithra ("Friend"), about whom a great light shone when he was born. In India over 5,000 years ago when Devakī gave birth at midnight to Krishna, a divine incarnation, the whole world was "irradiate with joy."

Jesus is spoken of as having been born of a "virgin" mother because spirit has no parent. The concept of an immaculate conception is purely mystical and symbolic, and has at least two applications: the one, referring to the initiate who is "born *from himself*," that is to the "birth of the Christ in man from the virgin-part of one's being, i.e., from the spiritual or highest portions of man's constitution"; the other referring to the cosmic virgin, "the Virgin-Mother of Space giving birth through her Child, the Cosmic Logos, to her multitudes of children of various kinds."†

As for the Magi or wise men: the Gospels don't tell us their names or what country they came from, or even how

---

*"Hávamál," §137, *The Masks of Odin* by Elsa-Brita Titchenell, p. 126.

†G. de Purucker, *The Esoteric Tradition* 2:1104-5.

many there were. In Western Europe most countries celebrate the coming of Three Kings at Epiphany, on January 6th. Some say they traveled from Persia and that is why they were called *Magi*, meaning "great" in wisdom. Others, like Augustine, believed that twelve wise men followed the star. Somewhere along the line names were attached: Melchior, Caspar (or Kaspar), and Balthasar. Purucker equates them with three of the seven sacred planets: Melchior with Venus, his casket of gold representing the light that Jesus was to shed upon the world; Caspar who carried myrrh "in a gold-mounted horn," with Mercury; and Balthasar, who offered frankincense, "pure incense," with the Moon.* It would appear that the wise men bringing gifts are symbolic of qualities which Jesus would need in order to bring to birth the Christos.

And the star? According to the German astronomer Kepler (1571–1630), while he was observing a rare grouping of planets, Mars, Jupiter, and Saturn in October 1604, he was startled to find a *stella nova* or "new star" (a nova or supernova, an exploding star) which remained brilliantly visible for seventeen months. Kepler concluded that what the Chinese astronomers had recorded as novae, both in 5 and 4 BC, gave credence to his view that the Star of Bethlehem may well have been a conjunction of two phenomena: a syzygy or planetary grouping of Mars, Jupiter, and Saturn in early 6 BC and the explosive light discharge that surrounds the "death" of an old star. May we not suggest, then, that the so-called Star of Bethlehem could

---

*Ibid. 2:1105–7.

have been a grouping of planets in the direction of the sun, enabling an initiant to pass in consciousness to the sun in the stellar deeps?

When we investigate the oral and scriptural traditions of other peoples, we discover that Jesus was not the *only* Son of God, but that his "miraculous" birth and death, his descent "to those in Hades as well as to all in earth" (Clement of Alexandria), were experienced by many saviors. All were *monogenēs* (only begotten), though not in the usual understanding of the phrase as the one and only Son of God, for we are all gods, sons of the divine. The splendor rests not in their uniqueness, in that each of them was one among the many who were and will in future cycles be "singly born," brought to birth alone from their own solar, divine source. All are members of that sacred community of "Sons of the Sun," Anointed Ones who periodically incarnate on earth to help us, "spirits in prison,"* free ourselves from our self-made bonds. But it is we who must turn the eyes of our souls toward the light: there is no liberation, no salvation, except that which is self-won.

Death by violence, burial in an underground tomb, bodily resurrection and ascension into heaven: what has all this to do with us today? Should we take this procession of events as having physically happened? Or should we see in the parallel mystical experience of so many world teachers a Mystery-teaching — the ultimate initiatory ordeal that every aspirant for communion and ultimate union with his inner god must undergo? How else could they claim one-

---

*1 Peter 3:19.

ness with divinity except by offering on the cross of self all that is less than godlike, except by descent into and triumph over the underworld of earth and of former thought habits, and by resurrection from the tomb of humanhood to shine forth in godhood? And the consummation? In the tradition of sun gods and saviors, such a one returns willingly to fulfill his sacred task, so that the ideals of compassion and of spiritual mastery may once again inspire human souls to nobler ends.

How may we interpret Jesus' death which he foretold, and his betrayal by Judas? Was it a betrayal as ordinarily understood? Or is there another level of meaning to this part of the Gospel narrative? Could it be that Judas was used as an instrument to carry out what had to be, foreordained by the karma of humanity, by the karma of Judas, as well as of Jesus? Be this as it may, Jesus knew that his "time was at hand," and that the Son of man must return to the Father.

Ascending the Garden of Gethsemane with Peter, John, and James, Jesus asked his disciples to sit awhile, and he went off to pray alone. Here was a more subtle "betrayal," or rather "failure" on the part of the very ones he had selected to stand guard in his moment of greatest need. Not a conscious failure, yet it carries a poignant lesson to us today, for how often in our individual strivings do we lack the selflessness of resolve, of love, to follow through. He said to his disciples: "My soul is exceeding sorrowful, even unto death: tarry ye here, and watch with me." Jesus then moved on farther and knelt, offering all that he was to his Father: "If it be possible, let this cup pass from me: nevertheless not as I will, but as thou wilt." When he returned he found his disciples heavy with sleep. "What, could ye not watch with me one hour?" Again Jesus said to them: "Watch and pray, that ye enter not into temptation: the spirit indeed is willing, but the flesh is weak." A second time he prayed, and once more the disciples slept. Even the third time, those who had given their utmost in devotion "betrayed" their Master, their strength not being sufficient. "Sleep on now, and take your rest: behold, the hour is at hand, and the Son of man is betrayed into the hands of sinners" (*Matthew* 26:37–45).

Though different in externals, a telling parallel to the Gethsemane scene is found in the "Book of the Great Passing," a Buddhist *Sutta* giving the essentials of Buddha's teaching during the final months of his life. The Pāli text narrates several conversations the Tathāgata had had with Ānanda, his faithful friend and disciple. He told Ānanda that should he desire it, the Tathāgata could "remain in the same birth for a kalpa, or for that portion of the kalpa which had yet to run." The hint was there, but it passed Ānanda by. Twice more the hint was given, but still Ānanda was oblivious to the momentous implication that, if the claim upon the Compassionate One was powerful enough, he could "remain during the kalpa . . . out of pity for the world, for the good and the gain and the weal of gods and men!"*

Shortly thereafter Māra the Tempter — the name means "death" — approached the Tathāgata, saying it was time for him to die and enter the nirvana he had renounced, for the

---

*Mahā-Parinibbāna-Sutta, ch. 3, §§3–4, Sacred Books of the East 11:41.

resolve he had earlier made had been fulfilled. At that time the Tathāgata had told Māra he would not die until the brethren and sisters and lay-disciples of both sexes shall have become "wise and well-trained, ready and learned, . . . [and] when others start vain doctrine, shall be able by the truth to vanquish and refute it, and so to spread the wonder-working truth abroad!"* Since Ānanda had made no call upon the Buddha to live on, the Tathāgata said to Māra: "make thyself happy, the final extinction of the Tathāgata shall take place before long. At the end of three months from this time the Tathāgata will die!" Whereupon there "arose a mighty earthquake, awful and terrible, and the thunders of heaven burst forth"† — not unlike what occurred during the "crucifixion" of Jesus when, from the sixth to the ninth hour darkness was upon the land, and after he had given up his spirit "the veil of the temple was rent in twain from the top to the bottom; and the earth did quake . . ." (*Matthew* 27:51).

Only later, when Ānanda had questioned the Buddha about the "mighty earthquake," did his disciple, in a flash, wake up. Only then, at the sudden realization that his beloved friend and mentor was soon to leave them, did Ānanda urge the Blessed One to live on through the kalpa "for the good and the happiness of the great multitudes." Three times he pleaded thus. The reply was inevitable: "Enough now, Ānanda, beseech not the Tathāgata! The time for making such request is past."‡ Had Ānanda bestirred him-

---

*Ibid., ch. 3, §7, p. 43.
†Ibid., ch. 3, §§9–10, p. 44.
‡Ibid., ch. 3, §§49–50, p. 54.

self at least by the third time, his teacher added, his wish would have been granted. In actuality, Buddha had spoken of this possibility on many previous occasions, yet each time Ānanda had let the hint go by unheeded.

This is not to suggest that had either Ānanda or the disciples of Jesus grasped the significance of the divine happenings surrounding their teachers, they could have forestalled the course of destiny. Even if there is scant historic fact in the Christian and Buddhist accounts, this does not negate the psychological truths they imbody. Neither story ends "happily ever after"; nor should it, for life is a blend of good and ill, of joy and sorrow, from which we may distill a tincture of wisdom.

If we find tragedy here, it is from viewing the events at too close range. From the perspective of many lives there is neither failure nor success, only learning experiences, and in this there is comfort as well as challenge. Peter, James, and John, and Ānanda too, are ourselves; we can identify with them, for their frailty is ours. How often we awake to the reality of a situation only after an experience, aware too late of an opportunity missed. Opportunities come and go for us all. Some we seize, almost by intuition, and are the gainer; others, at times important ones, we let slip through our fingers. Yet all is not lost as some part of our consciousness does register the lesson; were it otherwise, we would not wake up later, whether after a few hours or, perchance, not until the better part of our life has gone by. But wake up we do, ultimately, and this is the triumph.

In the case of Jesus, the very betrayal or failure on the

part of the disciples, though quite unconscious, would seem to have been an essential requisite for the law to be fulfilled, i.e., to allow for the consummation of the supreme initiatory trial of Jesus the man, when the human soul must stand alone, without protection of disciple or friend, and win. The human soul must be born as the Christ-sun without help other than from itself, its inbuilt reserve of solar strength. "Except a man be born again, he cannot see the kingdom of God" (*John* 3:3). Jesus is said to have experienced this *second* birth, a birth of the spirit, around the time of the winter solstice.

III

The cryptic words of the Apostles' Creed portray the despair and triumph of the man-Jesus become Christ: "crucified, dead and buried: he descended into hell; the third day he rose from the dead: he ascended to heaven." Whether Jesus was physically crucified remains an open question. The "crucifixion" may well be a symbol, an allegory told in order to portray the Christ-spirit crucified in matter: when the material, domineering side of human nature takes precedence in a life, it crucifies the spirit.

When the Christ came, he gave of his light, of his truth, but only a few comprehended. The rest did not understand and so, as the Gospels record, Jesus was tried and sentenced by Pontius Pilate. Of the supreme moment, when Jesus on the cross of matter is forsaken by all but his own self-disciplined soul, *Matthew* records the following:

> And about the ninth hour Jesus cried with a loud voice, Ēlī, Ēlī, lāma sabachthānī, that is to say, My God, my God, why hast thou forsaken me? — 27:46

In the translation the significance of this Hebrew phrase, inserted in the Greek original, is obscured. In reality, we have what amounts to two cries: the one of agony, the other of exaltation. The last Hebrew word, *sabachthānī* does *not* mean to forsake or abandon as the King James Version has it; on the contrary, it means to glorify, to bring peace, to raise in triumph. Yet the Greek text immediately "explains" it as "My God, my God, why hast thou forsaken me?" — which actually is a direct translation of the well-known cry of David in Psalm 22, *'Ēlī, 'Ēlī, lāmāh 'azabthānī*, the final word indeed meaning "to forsake."

What is the reason for this? It has been suggested that *Matthew* and *Mark* may have intentionally confused the matter in order to conceal (and yet reveal for those having eyes to see) what was in fact a Mystery-teaching. In short, the Greek "explanation" of the Hebrew phrase, quoting from the psalm, records the anguish felt by the *human* part of Jesus when in utter loneliness he had to face the dread regions of the netherworld and conquer all. Conversely, the Hebrew cry as preserved in *Matthew* and *Mark* was a cry of the Christos, Jesus triumphant: "O my God, how thou hast glorified me, how thou hast brought me out of darkness into the light!"*

---

*The author is indebted to G. de Purucker, *The Esoteric Tradition* 1:69–75; also to Ralston Skinner, *The Source of Measures*, pp. 300–301, and "No Error" by JRS (Skinner) in H. P. Blavatsky, *Collected Writings* 9:276–9, with corroborative "Note" by HPB on p. 279.

The Christ, let us say, was crucified. He was buried in the tomb and after three days he rose from the dead and ascended to heaven. That is the dogma of the Creed. It is also the story of initiation, which means the testing of the soul in great extremity to see whether it is sufficiently stalwart and selfless to undergo the most severe trials of the material world and come out whole, purified. Jesus rose from the underworld of initiation, the tomb of matter, glorified. United with the divinity within him, he ascended to his Father and became one with the universal divine force. He was no longer just a human being, having all our ordinary troubles caused by selfishness and greed. Jesus now was Christos, one "anointed" with the sacred oil, and a Son of God because the god within him had flooded the whole of his being with light.

The early Christians knew that the Christ mystery was not unique, something that had never occurred before, but was in very truth the culmination for their time of one of the most wondrous experiences possible to man. They understood that when Jesus became Christ he had successfully opened the pathway between the sun in his heart and the sun in the universe, and that the rays of the real Sun, which is a divinity, shone fully upon him: Jesus became as a sun god, in truth a "Son of the Sun."

This expression contains a profound mystical truth. It was and is used for the noblest among those whose natures have become so pure that they reflect clearly the light of the sun. In the ancient world the sun was called the Father of all, including the planets, our earth, and human beings. It was also believed that animating the sun we see in the sky is a great and shining divinity. The Romans called it Sol Invictus, the Unconquered Sun; the Greeks honored it as Apollo; the Phrygians as Attis (Atys). The Egyptians had their Osiris and Horus.

In the ancient world the peoples around the Mediterranean Basin held in reverence the Mystery-truth that when a man had completely conquered the base tendencies of his nature, the sun god within him had risen. We recall a verse from an old hymn by John of Damascus (675–749) which is still in use in both the Anglican and Greek Orthodox service:

>'Tis the spring of souls today:
>Christ hath burst His prison,
>And from three days' sleep in death
>As a sun hath risen.

Sun god of Christendom, Christ-Jesus illumined for his time the Way that had been hallowed by a long line of saviors before him.

10

Western Occultism

THE INTERMINGLING OF CULTURAL and religious traditions taking place today is exerting a profound influence on our thinking and mores. Just as Western methods and thought habits have left their energizing and often disruptive mark on the Orient, just so has the influx of Eastern ideas and rituals affected the thinking and habitual attitudes of thousands throughout Europe and America. As a result, huge cracks are forming in entrenched attitudes. In the West this is due to exposure to the philosophical and psychophysical disciplines of India, Tibet, China, and Japan; also in part to the growing interest in the rites and sacred lore of traditional peoples of the Americas, Australasia, and Africa. Even though the accent is largely on the "occult arts" (the mere overlay of genuine occultism), already a distinct change is taking place. From being strictly matter-dominated in outlook, we are coming to recognize spirit/consciousness/energy as the causal basis of *all* life, from the microworld of the atom to the macroworld of the cosmos, and all in between.

The entry into Western thought, from the 1780s on, of the profound metaphysical scriptures of the East was effected in the main by British civil servants in India. They were encouraged by the then Governor-General, Warren Hastings, to study Sanskrit and allied languages so that they might better understand what moved the Hindu soul. So impressed were a few of these officials that they began to translate the great epics of India, the *Rāmāyaṇa* and *Mahābhārata*, especially the *Bhagavad-Gītā*, as well as the Upanishads. In 1785 Sir Charles Wilkins published the first English translation of the *Gītā* in London — incredible that we in the West have known of its existence for little more than two hundred years. With similar translation work in process in France and Germany, the philosophic treasury of the East gradually infiltrated the thought consciousness of the Occident.

At that time there was a rather sharp demarcation between the scholarly elite and the great majority who were academically untrained and therefore remained largely unaware of the intellectual and spiritual impact of these emancipating ideas. The dissemination of theosophy from 1875 on, along with the publication of inexpensive editions of the *Gītā* and Patañjali's *Yoga Sūtras*, was the needed catalyst to leaven the popular as well as the scientific and philosophic thinking of Western culture.

Nowadays the concepts of karma and reincarnation, the oneness of man and nature, the physical world as but a transient appearance of the Real, and the possibility of communion with the source of Being by anyone willing and able to undergo the discipline — all these are becoming a familiar part of Western thought. With hatha yoga, meditation techniques, and other Oriental methods of self-culture rapidly being adapted to the Occidental temperament, one can only agree with W. Q. Judge's prophetic comment that a type of "Western Occultism" is already in the making.

There are both positive and negative aspects to all of this, as is only natural with any innovation, particularly of spiritual and intellectual import. Some of these may not be easy to distinguish, as their side effects may take years to become fully apparent. Just because a teaching or ceremonial is old or hails from the Orient is of itself neither a warranty nor a denial of its spiritual worth. Hence, everything we see or hear must pass the test of our *inner* touchstone. This will be increasingly necessary in the future as the longing for self-transcendence exercises the minds of a growing number of earnest seekers. Among the multiplicity of courses in self-culture being offered today in seminars, workshops, and retreats, a good many hold out the promise of self-transformation in weeks. All that is required, we are told, is to sit for so many minutes and recite a mantra or listen to a tape recording with a subliminal or overt message, and peace of mind, relaxation from tension, oneness with cosmic consciousness, and restoration of bodily health will be ours!

Perhaps this is because a number of present-day gurus have found many in the West looking not so much for a means of turning inward as for a type of religion that will improve the externals of living. The real question is: What is the motive behind the urge for self-transcendence, for self-identification with our source? Should we not offer something of ourselves for the privilege of "serenity, peace of heart, oneness with the All"? No one can know the inner motivation of another, but we should examine our own motives as far as we can determine them. What stands out in much of the current absorption, not only in imported Oriental systems but also in Occidental self-actualization programs, is the "for oneself" approach — a trend that is diametrically opposed to the path of compassion.

It is well to recall that in the ancient Greek Mysteries the stages of the initiatory process were variously enumerated, often broadly as three: *katharsis*, cleansing, purification of the soul; *muēsis*, testing or trial of the candidate, to prove integrity of motive and firmness of will; and third, if successful, *epopteia*, revelation, i.e., "seeing" behind the veil of nature. Always the character had to be shaped in accordance with the noblest ideals; nothing was gained without sacrifice. Except the seed of self die, the soul-plant cannot take birth.

True occultism — which is altruism lived, combined with knowledge of the inner structure of man and the universe — demands of its followers complete purity of thought and of deed, and the utmost in self-mastery. In the esoteric cycle of learning and discipline, the neophyte is enjoined first to absorb as far as he is able the ideal of self-forgetfulness and love for all beings. Only after he has thoroughly understood that thought for others before oneself is expected of him, is he permitted to direct his attention to high philosophy: "Live the life, and you will know the doctrine." Before entering upon any specialized training program we should examine our inner motives to be certain that the course we have in mind is one our higher self would approve.

Self-transcendence, if it is to be lasting, is not obtained by external means alone. It occurs without formality, in the still recesses of one's inmost self. Moreover, as the teachings and the path they illumine enter ever more deeply into the core of our being, we progressively grow and learn. No exoteric training in self-transformation can match the inner transmutation of soul quality that takes place in the silence, the effects of which endure beyond death. They endure because they are registered in our *spiritual* nature.

To work from without inwards may produce certain results fairly quickly, but as they seldom reach higher than the mental and emotional aspects of our nature they will be short-lived. When our thoughts and feelings are other-centered, they build solid spiritual character traits that will outlast the cycles. Simply put, when our primary concern is wholehearted devotion to the ideal and practice of *brotherhood* so that eventually it is universally lived — if we can cling to this goal, it will be our lifeline to esoteric reality.

Ideas such as these give a fresh perspective on many trends that are gaining popularity. Yoga, for example, is almost commonplace in the West, haṭha yoga in its simpler forms being the most popular. Yoga means "union," from the Sanskrit verb *yuj*, "to join, to unite, to yoke." It referred originally, and still does in its pure sense, to the quest for union of the soul with the divine within: the *unio mystica* or mystical union of the early Christians and medieval mystics who sought to attain unison of soul with the Divine or God-image within.

There are many types of yoga, and these appeal to different temperaments: *bhakti yoga*, "yoga of devotion"; *karma yoga*, "yoga of action"; *jñāna yoga*, "yoga of knowledge"; and others. The path of *rāja yoga** is the "royal or kingly union" of the personal self with the illumined self. It is of small consequence what path we take outwardly, so long as we set our inner goal on the highest within. "In whatever way men approach me, in that way do I assist them; but whatever the path taken by mankind, that path is mine."†

Today in the West there are many practitioners of yoga whose goal is to restore physical health and alleviate, where possible, some of the unusually stressful conditions people are experiencing in these crucial times. We would be well advised, however, to stop short before undertaking sophisticated breathing and other techniques that could, if unwisely pursued, interfere with the proper functioning of the *prāṇas*. Prāṇa is a Sanskrit term for the five or seven "life-breaths" that circulate through and maintain the body in health.

The Chinese for centuries have taught that sound physical and psychic health depends upon the balance of yin and yang. If one, however unknowingly, upsets the natural rhythmic flow of the *ch'i* — their term for prāṇa — through the twelve primary meridians or energy channels of the body, imbalance of the yin/yang may result. In other words, when there is interference with the natural lines of force, a misalignment of prāṇic balance may occur, often with serious consequences. Rather than concentrate on the psychic and physical aspects of the constitution, far better to

---

*See *Bhagavad-Gītā* 9:2, the first line of which reads: *rājavidyā rājaguhyaṃ*, literally "royal knowledge, royal mystery."
†Ibid. 4:11 (Judge recension, p. 24).

focus attention on the spiritual and higher mental and moral faculties. When inner balance is achieved and normal health measures are observed, the physical will in time follow suit (unless, as may happen, stronger karmic impediments must be worked through).

Much emphasis also is placed on finding one's inner center, and rightly so. This centering of oneself is a private individual process of "self-naughting," self-stripping, as the mystics call it, emptying the nature of externals and becoming one with our essential self. It may take a lifetime, or several lifetimes, to achieve in fullness — no outer circumstances will be as effective as "losing the self that we may find the self."

Since the 1960s groups have sprung up all over the world sponsoring self-transcendence courses that offer various methods of achieving alternative states of consciousness: how to rouse the *kuṇḍalinī* or "serpent fire" seated near the base of the spine; how to activate the chakras, how to meditate by focusing on a triangle, candle flame, crystal, lighted bulb, or by repetition of a mantra. These and other psycho-physical practices are carried out in the hope of attaining nirvanic consciousness. I would not advocate any of these methods, not because they are essentially faulty, but because they can prove deleterious on account of our ingrained selfish proclivities.

Today the hunger for new and better ways to live is very strong. People long to find meaning in a seemingly meaningless succession of crises and are experimenting with alternative routes, anything that is different from what they grew up with. This is part of the spiritual and psychic awakening going on worldwide, but to adopt without careful screening any method of self-development, especially those that promise instant results, is a high-risk venture. Where there is instability in the character (and who of us is perfectly pure in heart and in motive?), the invasion of our psyche by baneful influences from the lowest levels of the astral light could be detrimental both to physical and mental health. Besides, concentration of mental and psychic energy on the transient elements of the nature has the drawback of diverting attention away from essentials to externals. This cannot have the beneficial effect that the altruistic and nonself-centered approach of rāja yoga has on the aspirant. All of this is old wisdom which many today are beginning to intuit and apply to their lives.

In the *Bhagavad-Gītā* there is a phrase: *ātmānam ātmanā paśya* — "see the self by means of the self." This may be interpreted in two ways: see the limited self, the personality, by means of the glowing self or ātman within; or, see the ātman within, the light of the true self, by means of the awakening personal self. The ideal is to have an unimpeded flow of energy, of consciousness, between our ātmic source and the personality. When we seek first to offer ourselves to the noblest within, we quicken the fires of our highest chakra, the ātmic center, which in turn will radiate its influence on all the other chakras.

Viewing the seven principles of the human constitution as a pillar of light, each principle being sevenfold, supposing we try to reach to ātman, we may fairly soon reach the subātman of our psychic center. But if we have concentrated too pointedly on that level there is every possibility with certain natures, not only of becoming deflected from our goal but, unhappily, of getting our principles out of alignment.

If without strain or any sense of pride we offer ourself deeply and sincerely in the service of our inmost self, then the light from the highest ātman — the ātmic subprinciple of our ātman — will illumine our whole being from above downwards. We will remain in alignment because our psychic and intellectual and other centers will be irradiated with the supreme ātmic light, and there will be a transforming influence on our lives.

The popularization of meditation practices in the West has had certain positive results and helped many to handle their deep-seated anxieties. Stilling the mind and calming the emotions for a few moments every day is therapeutic: by deliberately dropping our worries, we become free inwardly and can refocus ourselves for our life's task. On the other hand, high-powered promotion of meditation may be self-defeating. For example, one is put off at the start when money is charged for a mantra that purports to raise one to cosmic awareness. No one *needs* a mantra in order to lift his consciousness unto the hills of the spirit and receive the benediction of momentary communion with the highest within.

There are ways and ways to meditate, and ways and ways to attain a higher awareness. When we become inwardly still, our inner voice may be heard in those quiet yet clear intimations that move the soul. Every night upon retiring we can open the way for the intuition by stripping the nature of all resentments and irritations, ridding the heart of all arrogant and unkind thoughts and feelings about others. If we have slipped a little during the day, let us acknowledge it with the will to do better. We then enter into harmony with our real self, and the consciousness is freed to go where it will. This is a mystery which we do not really understand, but the wonder is that in the morning we wake up refreshed in spirit, with a new and warmer feeling for others, and often with answers to perplexing questions.

To follow this simple practice is restorative on all planes, and we will be adding to rather than detracting from the harmony of our surroundings. Whatever course of self-betterment one pursues, sacrifice is required: we cannot hope to gain access to the higher realms of being if we have not earned the right of entry. Only those who come clean of anger, resentment, and selfish desire are fit recipients of the keys to nature's wisdom. To expect otherwise is to run the risk of opening the door to elemental forces of a low kind that may be difficult to eject from the consciousness. Prayer, aspiration, meditation *are* effective in that they set up a vibratory response throughout all nature; the more ardent the aspirant, the greater power do they have to activate noble (or ignoble) energies both within the individual and in the auric envelope surrounding earth.

True meditation is true aspiration, a "breathing toward" the divine, an elevating of the mind and heart toward the highest and, as such, is as essential for the soul as food is for the body. If we would orient our lives toward the light emanating from our inner god, we must aspire; but let us be careful in our intensity not to be led into blind alleys of a self-seeking nature which tend to focus attention on our own advancement, our own stature and achievements. After all, where we stand — spiritually or otherwise — is of small moment compared to the quality of our contribution to the whole. The real issue is: Are we giving the best of ourselves to this world so that we bring warmth and courage instead of chill and gloom to our surroundings?

Meister Eckhart, 14th-century mystic, whose purity of life gives luster to his instructions and sermons even today, put it eloquently:

> If some one were in a rapture like Saint Paul's, and there were a sick man needing help, it would be better to come out of the rapture and exercise practical love by serving the one in need. . . .
>
> In this life no man reaches the point at which he can be excused from practical service.*

The finest type of meditation is a turning of the soul toward the light within in aspiration to be of greater service, without exaggerated longing for some special revelation. Any method of meditation that helps us to lessen our self-centeredness is beneficial; if it increases egocentricity, it is harmful.

It is indeed our duty to search for truth, wherever it may be; also, to use our keenest discrimination in every circumstance, appreciative of worth yet alert for falsity, knowing that every human being has the inalienable right to follow the path which seems best to him. In reality, the only pathway we can follow is the one we unfold from within ourself

---

*Sheldon Cheney, *Men Who Have Walked with God*, p. 194; cf. *Meister Eckhart, A Modern Translation*, trans. Raymond Bernard Blakney, p. 14.

as we seek to evolve and self-become what we inwardly are.

Just as the spider spins from itself the silken threads that are to form its web, so do we unfold from the depths of our being the very path that is ours. Our challenge is to heed the mandates of our inner selfhood over and above the external pulls; if we don't, we hurt ourselves — and others too — until we learn. At times those mandates call for a quality of self-discipline and courage we are not accustomed to, and the sacrifice of things we hold dear. But all that is offered in sacrifice is as nothing compared to what we in our innermost self long for.

The most fruitful meditation, therefore, is an absorption of thought and aspiration in the noblest ideal we can envision. We will not need to worry about specific postures, techniques, or gurus; there will be a natural inflow of light into the nature, for our inner master, our real guru, is our Self.

Psychism

WITH THE SPIRITUAL AWAKENING that is taking place, there is an urgency to probe the deeper and normally unconscious levels of the human psyche. At one end of the spectrum we find brilliant thinkers, in every discipline of inquiry, breaking the matter barrier and exploring new dimensions of awareness, of soul/mind/body interaction. Their goal is to develop a new model for man as a planetary being in a universe recognized as his native home. Along with this is a grassroots cry for recognition of earth as our mother, for an ecology of mind and spirit and body, for acceptance of holistic approaches to healing and medicine along with enlightened care of the aged, ill, and dying, and also of the mentally and emotionally disturbed. At the other end of the spectrum, purveyors of psychic baubles lure thousands with glamorous offers of "a direct route to ultimate power" and the like.

In the middle range is the rapidly increasing number of individuals and organizations sponsoring all manner of retreats, seminars, and workshops in psychophysiological practices: withdrawal of the senses, self-regulation procedures, cleansing of psychic blockages, energizing techniques, dream evaluation and control, stress and tension management, and scores of "therapies" as experiential aids to participating in alternative levels of consciousness. Many become confused and are unable to recognize that which is of permanent value.

To be forewarned is to be forearmed: as long as we are attentive and responsible, and test by our inner touchstone the truth or falsity of whatever comes before us, there is no real cause for fear. But it is imperative that we keep the reins of decision in our own hands and discover for ourselves in which direction this or that "path" or "promise" or "initiation" is leading us: to emancipation of the soul, or to vanity and worse confusion of goals. To be sure, at every frontier there are perils, and where the frontiers verge on astral planes of our constitution and that of our globe, the greater is the need for vigilance. Since we are dealing here primarily with nonphysical dimensions, a larger measure of discrimination is required.

The first requisite is to know what we are dealing with. What do we mean by "astral"? Originally from the Greek — *astron*, "star" — the term was used by Medieval and Renaissance philosophers, Alchemists, and Hermetists for the subtle, invisible substance that encloses and penetrates our physical earth. Paracelsus refers to it as the Sidereal Light, and Éliphas Lévi called it the serpent or dragon whose emanations often plague humanity. The Upanishads of India use the term *ākāśa*, "shining," for the luminous substance that pervades the whole of space, sun and moon, lightning and stars, as well as the self (ātman) of man. The Stoic philosophers had their quintessence, "fifth essence," or aether from which the lower four elements derive, and the Latins their *anima mundi*, "soul of the world," which they conceived as surrounding and vivifying all beings. To most peoples of earlier times the celestial bodies, stars, and planets, were "animals" — living beings filled with the "breath" (*anima, spiritus*) of life. They were gods using stellar and planetary bodies as their means of gaining experience, each having its *nous* and *psyche* (its noetic and psychical aspects, its spirit and soul). There was never any question in the minds of those schooled in the Mysteries about the intimate and continuing interconnection of man and nature.

In modern theosophy the term "astral" is used for the subtle model on which the physical bodies of both man and globe build themselves. Today the word astral is frequently found in parapsychology journals, although various terms are likewise employed, such as energy body, bioplasma, and the like.

The astral light, as earth's finer counterpart is called in theosophical parlance, ranges from the most dense to the most ethereal and spiritual, its lowest levels being heavy with the dregs of human thought and emotion, its uppermost levels merging with the ākāśa through which higher beings may commune at rare intervals with those who command their interest. H. P. Blavatsky refers to the astral light as "the great picture-gallery of eternity" because it contains "a faithful record of every act, and even thought, of man, of all that was, is, or ever will be, in the phenomenal Universe."[*]

Since whatever is experienced leaves its seal on the earth's aura and on our own, the astral light is the repository

---

[*] *The Secret Doctrine* 1:104.

and hence the reflector of the most altruistic thoughts and aspirations as well as the most degraded of human impulses of the countless men and women who have ever lived on our planet. There is continual interchange: we imprint the astral light, and the astral light in turn leaves its imprint upon us, a two-way flow of astral energies circulating in and through earth and its kingdoms. Actually, we are awash with astral currents all the time: our thoughts are astral, our feelings also. As we talk together, we are using astral thought substance. When we are inwardly in harmony, we may unknowingly be the recipient of intimations of truth and beauty either from our inner god, or from the upper ranges of the astral light (ākāśa). Contrariwise, when we are depressed and allow negative thoughts and emotions to make inroads into our consciousness, we may be opening the door unawares to lower astral influences. Unless we are in command of ourselves, it is often downright hard to shut that door when we want to, and even more difficult to keep it shut. Moreover, to the undisciplined and untrained, the currents of the astral light can prove extremely deceptive, and therefore dangerous. Rashly to venture into astral and psychic experimentation, ignorant of the hazards involved and, most important, without the protection of an utterly stainless soul, is as foolhardy as to jump into quicksand.

In spite of admonitions against the potential misuse of our latent psychomental power, psychic manifestations among all types of people have notably increased in recent decades. In consequence, there has been a tremendous upsurge of interest in ESP, levitation, divination, crystal and pyramid power, psychokinesis, and all manner of astral busywork, so much so that we feel impelled to ask a few questions: Is it prudent in our present stage of evolution to force, as in a hothouse, the cultivation of paranormal faculties when we are still so very egocentric? Are we sufficiently prepared by inner purity and self-mastery to deal with astral forces that heretofore have been held in check by nature's protective closure of our physical senses to octaves beyond the normal range?

What of channeling, the much talked about "gift" of mediumship? Hardly a gift, for to be a medium for the channeling of messages from beings from the "other side" may seem to serve us well for a while, yet it often happens that the receiver in time becomes prey to external forces beyond his control. Our psychiatric wards in hospitals and prisons tell the harrowing story of the many thousands of unhappy victims of psychic possession. Yet, to be a channel is an everyday occurrence. We are, each of us, constantly the channel or recipient of thoughts and atmospheres that arise in ourself or among family, friends, neighbors, our nation, and humanity as a whole. Inevitably so. Could we not on occasion be the channel for an inspiration that we, usually in spite of our ordinary mind, hear, see, or feel, when momentarily we have become a transmitter of light and inspiration from the ākāśic heights? There is nothing remarkable about this; it has been going on for millennia, in every land among all peoples. But this is a far cry from the type of channeling that captures headlines.

On the other hand, what of those who commit heinous acts: many scarcely know why, or what may have impelled them to murder or rape. Did inherent weakness of will allow the ingress into their psyche of malevolent forces from the lowest portions of the astral light? While nature utilizes all things for ultimate good, and broader insights may well come through at times, channeling could deflect many sincere seekers from their true goal and, at worst, plunge them into a psychic whirlpool of confusion and, possibly, into unconscious sorcery.

We can take a lesson from Macbeth: almost immediately, on learning from the witches of Endor that he is to be Thane of Cawdor, he becomes anxious. Will all really be as they foretell? Observing Macbeth in severe stress of emotion, swinging between greed and fear, Banquo muses:

> But 'tis strange:
> And oftentimes, to win us to our harm,
> The instruments of darkness tell us truths,
> Win us with honest trifles, to betray's
> In deepest consequence.
> — *Macbeth*, Act I, scene iii

This is precisely what happens to many recipients of "messages" from those "beyond." Astral entities channeled by mediums in the beginning often do win us with honest trifles, certain small truths, which lead us on, only to betray us later in matters of deepest consequence.

Then there are those who are interested in "astral travel," getting out of the body and trying to reach their ātman; or to visit people, other lands, planets, or planes astrally. Many sincerely believe they can help friends or relatives in this manner. To understand why this is not a wise way of attaining union with one's ātman or divine self, we need a knowledge of the sevenfold nature of human consciousness: the divine, the spiritual, and the higher mind, the lower mind combined with the desire principle, and the vital, astral, and physical. The desire/mental part of man forms our ordinary personal self, and when illumined by the intuitional and higher mind, we have an awakened soul. Soul is a rather broad term that can be used for many aspects of our being. Usually the Greeks spoke of *nous* as the higher mind, the higher intelligence, and of *psyche*, daughter of nous, as the soul.

To take a dogmatic stance, however, and condemn out of hand all extranormal phenomena is as shortsighted as to endorse everything astral or psychic. Judgment is required: the wisdom of ages has shown that to open wide the entrance into astral realms is tantamount to opening a Pandora's box of elemental energies, both benign and malignant. We caution against deviation from altruistic intent because in any astral dealings, however innocent the motive may be at the start, the excitement of easy success too often leads to corrosion of moral principle. Human nature is ever susceptible to appeals to self-benefit; the more disguised they are, the greater the need for caution, lest unawares the seed of pride germinate. Psychic vanity in many and strange forms constitutes a most seductive snare, binding the aspirations to the personal level instead of freeing them to respond to the call of one's deepest being.

There are of course many degrees of psychic or astral involvement. As noted earlier, we use nonphysical power all the time: love, hate, thought, and emotion of every kind are manifestations of psychic or spiritual faculties. Most people, moreover, are naturally telepathic, experiencing thought-transference more often than they realize, especially with those close to them. Then there are the sensitives, who have a sort of sixth sense which, when manifesting unsought and in a completely natural way, is often a protection for others and for themselves. But when these powers are sought out of vanity, as a self-indulgence, or a running away from the discipline of daily responsibility, they readily become a danger. Those who have a "spirit guide," who prate about hearing the "bells," or through automatic writing receive the "most wonderful teachings," should be wary, lest what they are "seeing" or "hearing" may not be wisdom "from above, but is earthly" (*James* 3:15); or be as candlelight compared to the brilliance of the sun.

At the risk of oversimplification, let us draw a parallel between the fate of the alcoholic and the psychic addict. Before they realize what is happening, they have become "possessed" by a force outside of themselves which they feel powerless to control. Just as iron filings are drawn to lines of magnetic force, so are "elemental beings" from the astral body of earth attracted to whomever will give them an opening; and the lowest planes of the astral are weighted down with humanity's most evil thoughts. Fortunate are those whose pure goodness affords them protection, for they will respond only to that which is akin to them.

We find warnings in Buddhist writings against the improper use of our psychic faculties. In one of the texts of the Pāli Canon* an incident is reported of a merchant of Rājagaha who acquired a block of sandalwood and had a

---

*Cullavagga, V, 8:1–2, Sacred Books of the East, 20:78–81.

beautiful wooden bowl made from it. He challenged anyone claiming to be possessed of *iddhi*,* "power, craft, skill," to fetch it from the top of a very tall bamboo; if he succeeded the bowl would be his. Several toyed with the idea, but went no further. Finally the venerable monk Bhāradvāja came forward, and "rising up in the air, took the bowl, and went thrice" around Rājagaha. The villagers were ecstatic and began shouting and running after him. On learning the cause of this raucous behavior, the Buddha called the monks together. When Bhāradvāja stated that he had indeed retrieved the bowl by the use of iddhi, the Buddha said to him and the assembled monks:

> This is improper, Bhāradvāja, not according to rule, unsuitable, unworthy of a Samaṇa [recluse], unbecoming, and ought not to be done. How can you, Bhāradvāja, for the sake of a miserable wooden pot, display before the laity the superhuman quality of your miraculous power of Iddhi?
> — Ibid., p. 80

After this rebuke the Buddha discoursed on spiritual themes, and then stated to the assembled monks:

> You are not, O Bhikkhus, to display before the laity the superhuman power of Iddhi. Whosoever does so, shall be guilty of a dukkaṭa [an offense]. Break to pieces, O Bhikkhus, that wooden bowl; and when you have ground it to powder, give it to the Bhikkhus as perfume for their eye ointments. — Ibid., p. 81

---

*Pāli form of the Sanskrit *siddhi*. These are of two kinds: the one "embraces the lower, coarse, psychic and mental energies; the other ... exacts the highest training of Spiritual powers." — H. P. Blavatsky, *The Voice of the Silence*, p. 73.

Even if we faithfully adhere to the ancient proscription against improper use of paranormal powers, when the *pāramitās* ("transcendental virtues" — see ch. 13) are practiced with diligence over an extended period, profound inner changes do occur both in character and within the constitution. The individual may discover, especially in the practice of *dhyāna*, "meditation, concentration," that certain of the iddhis are activated. This is not out of line provided one maintains silence, inner balance, purity of motive, and vigilance against psychic vanity.

All of this HPB made amply clear in the Preliminary Memorandum and Rules she sent to applicants who sought to join the newly formed Esoteric Section (1888):

> the student — save in exceptional cases — will not be taught how to produce physical phenomena, nor will any magical powers be allowed to develop in him; nor, if possessing such powers naturally, will he be permitted to exercise them before he has thoroughly mastered the knowledge of SELF, . . . until he has in abeyance all his lower passions and his PERSONAL SELF . . .
>
> 9. No member shall pretend to the possession of psychic powers that he has not, nor boast of those which he may have developed. Envy, jealousy, and vanity are insidious and powerful foes to progress, and it is known from long experience that, among beginners especially, the boasting of, or calling attention to, their psychic powers almost invariably causes the development of these faults and increases them when present. Hence —
>
> 10. No member shall tell to another, especially to a fellow member, how much he has progressed or what recogni-

tion he has received, nor shall he by hints cause such to be known.*

While extranormal phenomena have a place under certain circumstances, they are only an outer expression of a more subtle condition. Providentially the great majority, in former times as well as today, have an inborn warning signal against inviting anything of a psychic nature into their lives: either out of a natural fear of the unknown, or because of having already gone this route in the present or a former life and found it to be a blind alley. With some the onset of hypersensitivity is spontaneous; with others it is induced by mind-training programs or drugs. Without question, at this convergence of cycles, when the Piscean age is on the way out and the Aquarian age is becoming the dominant influence globally, psychical manifestations are on the increase along with an intensified interest in and cultivation of once latent faculties. If a person is born with his psychic nature more or less developed, we should recognize it for what it is but not exaggerate its importance. Due in part to the thinning of the barrier between the physical and the astral, many more today, even very young children, are exhibiting psychic leanings.

H. P. Blavatsky foresaw that humanity was fast entering a "new cycle [where] the latent psychic and occult powers in man are beginning to germinate and grow." But, she added, "Understand once for all that there is nothing 'spiritual' or 'divine' in *any* of these manifestations."† In her fourth

---

E.S. Instructions III:4–5, pp. 21–2; reprinted in H. P. Blavatsky, *Collected Writings* 12:488, 495.

†*H. P. Blavatsky to the American Conventions: 1888–1891*, p. 28.

letter to the American theosophists written in April 1891, shortly before her death, she urged them to "watch therefore carefully this development, inevitable in your race and evolution-period, so that it may finally work for good and not for evil." Her warning is explicit:

> Psychism, with all its allurements and all its dangers, is necessarily developing among you, and you must beware lest the Psychic outruns the Manasic [mental] and Spiritual development. Psychic capacities held perfectly under control, checked and directed by the Manasic principle, are valuable aids in development. But these capacities running riot, controlling instead of controlled, using instead of being used, lead the Student into the most dangerous delusions and the certainty of moral destruction. — Ibid., p. 35

Notable, however, is the difference in emphasis in psychic interest today from what it was during the closing decades of the nineteenth century. At that time — leaving aside those who, as in all eras, are caught by the glamour of phenomena — only a relatively few of the more intrepid minds were attracted, for the scientific and cultured world for the most part frowned upon such doings. In the twentieth century, and particularly in its last decades, the potential of human consciousness specifically and paranormal phenomena in general have been subjected to controlled testing. Experimentation in these and allied areas is being conducted by neuroscientists and others in an effort to penetrate the inner layers of human consciousness. At the same time, some very dangerous research is going on. We have only to glance at current "metaphysical" magazines to realize how sinister is the trend of some of this research and resulting practices worldwide.

Fortunately, a number of researchers in the field are aware of inherent risks, particularly to those mentally and psychologically unstable. Some of them are speaking out strongly against "hypnotic programming," and warning against the psychic pollution to which hypnotized victims open themselves. We cannot emphasize too much the peril of putting oneself under the will or within the aura of another. It is not recommended; it is not advisable. We must be master of ourselves at all times; and to let ourselves even unconsciously slip under the dominance of another is to weaken by so much our innate power to handle our lives.

We human beings are here with an immense background of force, generated through lifetimes, which we are learning to direct along those paths of destiny that are rightfully ours. While we interact with one another and thereby affect to some degree each other's karma, no one — no god in heaven, no demon in hell, no Master or Adept — has the right to interfere with the inner life of any human being. Were we to permit another to impose his will upon ours and break into the citadel of our selfhood, we would be degrading our humanhood and prostituting the intent of our higher self.

Young people especially should be aware of the potential risk, because as the years go by they will be meeting with this type of intrusion more and more. Physical war is not nearly so hazardous as the control of wills and of minds which increasingly is taking more subtle forms. One day, and hopefully during the present century, war on the battlefield will be a nightmare of the past. However, we will need to maintain our vigilance, for conflict will be centered for the most part on the mental and psychological planes. Then as now there will be need for the courage and the determination to fend off subliminal darts that could pierce the inner fabric of our being.

How can we protect ourselves against psychic invasion? One certain protection is to be aware of the dangers, yet not afraid. When fear, real fear, threatens to take hold, if we trust fully our deepest being within, we will know that *nothing* can touch us, no entity or thing can injure our real self. "Perfect love casteth out fear." The love must be genuine, self-forgetful without conditions. Consistently orienting our consciousness in a selfless direction, with purity of motive, is a natural safeguard.

As we head into the future, we had best keep aware of the rapid changes in the consciousness field. It behooves us to understand the nature of our many-faceted constitution from physical to spiritual, and to recognize the imperative need for each of us to be master of our own decisions. By first strengthening our moral and spiritual faculties, our mental and psychic powers will develop proportionately; we shall be in a better position to use them wisely and for the benefit of all. The wisdom of ages is epitomized in Jesus' words: "Seek ye first the kingdom of God [of the spirit] . . . and all these things shall be added unto you."

Today the challenge before us is not how we can stop the tidal wave of psychic experimentation, but how we can help give it the needed upward direction so that it will "finally work for good and not for evil." The future is open-ended, with enormous possibilities both for progress and retrogression. What the generations to come will face we cannot foretell. Their dilemma and opportunity may well focus, even as ours does today, on how to prepare inwardly to achieve the required moral purity and strength of character to meet the continuing ingress into the thought atmosphere of our planet of astral and psychic influences — from within themselves, from others, and from the earth's astral light.

We ask again, why are so many interested in acquiring extrasensory powers? Of what benefit will this be to anyone? Suppose we do learn to mind-read, to travel in our astral body, see clairvoyantly, foretell the future, would anything of spiritual worth be gained? More to the point, and perhaps the only question: What is our real motivation in life? If we can answer this honestly, to the satisfaction of both intellect and intuition, we may find that we need to center our concern in our spirit-soul, where I and Thou are one — not in the psychic and physical, the least permanent parts of our constitution.

The building of character is an ongoing challenge: the transmutation of selfishness into altruism, of personal interest into the warmth of compassion — a slow, patient alchemy.

12

The Two Paths

NONE HAVE EXERTED SO PROFOUND an influence on the destiny of the human race as have the Illumined Ones — those who, on reaching omniscience, the bliss of nirvana, turn back from the heights to live in the foothills with their younger brothers still struggling in ignorance and confusion. Exemplars of the love they have generated over the aeons for all living beings, they belong to the sacred hierarchy of light and their sacrifice remains a beacon in the darkness of our lives.

> Compassion speaks and saith: "Can there be bliss when all that lives must suffer? Shalt thou be saved and hear the whole world cry?"
> The PATH is one, Disciple, yet in the end, twofold. Marked are its stages by four and seven Portals. At one end — bliss immediate, and at the other — bliss deferred. Both are of merit the reward: the choice is thine.
> — *The Voice of the Silence,* pp. 71, 41

In these fragments selected from the "Book of the Golden Precepts," HPB transmitted for the "daily use" of modern students the age-old teaching that from the first step to the last we are making choices and thereby shaping our character and the karma leading to this supreme choice. She devotes her *Voice of the Silence* to the choice between the two paths of spiritual discipline facing the "candidate for wisdom": the one of liberation, enlightenment for oneself, ending in nirvana with no further return to earth; the other, that of renunciation, a slower and more challenging path chosen by those who would follow the way of compassion exemplified by Buddhas and Christs. They, on attaining the light and peace of nirvanic wisdom, remember their fellow humans and return to inspire those who will heed to wake up and pursue the sacred quest.

This twofold path of spiritual endeavor is portrayed graphically in the Mahāyāna Buddhist tradition. The one path, *pratyeka-yāna*, "for oneself path," has for its aim nirvana, release from all that is nonspiritual and earthly. This is the course followed by those disciples, monks, and aspirants who seek enlightenment for self alone, private salvation and liberation from the endless cycle of birth and rebirth. Early Orientalists usually refer to the pratyeka as "private buddhas" because they pursue the goal singly and are not "teaching" buddhas. It is a "for-one" or private striving for nirvana, that demands consistency in focusing one's aspiration and effort toward self-mastery through purification of motive and control of body, speech, and mind. Still, by virtue of its *self*-centeredness, it is a path that is *self*-ish, for one's self. As stated in the *Voice* (pp. 43, 86), the pratyeka buddha "makes his obeisance but to his *Self*. . . . Caring nothing for the woes of mankind or to help it," he enters into the glory and the wisdom and the light of nirvana.

In the Pāli scripture *The Questions of King Milinda**

---

*Cf. IV, l, §§20–27, T. W. Rhys Davids trans., Sacred Books of the East 35:155–62.

"seven classes of minds" are delineated, the sixth being that of the pratyeka buddha, who seeks no teacher and lives alone "like the solitary horn of the rhinoceros."* His wisdom is only such as can be contained within "a shallow brook on his own property," whereas the wisdom of a perfect or complete buddha is like that of "the mighty ocean."

Another scripture calls the knowledge of a pratyeka buddha "limited," even though he is said to know everything about his previous births and deaths. In contrast, the complete or perfect buddhas or buddhas of compassion are omniscient, because when required they have command over the total resources of knowledge and can focus directly on "any point which they choose to remember, throughout many times ten million world-cycles," and thus discern instantaneously the exact truth of any situation, person, or event.†

Tsong-kha-pa of 14th-century Tibet was a transmitter of Buddha-wisdom. He spoke of pratyeka buddhas as Solitary Realizers of "middling" capacity: even though they persevere in their purpose, their merit and wisdom are limited because their efforts are "for their own sake alone" in contradistinction to the bodhisattva-become-buddha who bears "the altruistic mind of enlightenment at the very beginning."‡

The *amṛita-yāna*, "deathless path," although slower and

---

*Ibid., p. 158.

† *Visuddhi Magga* (Way of Purity) by Buddhaghosa; cited in *World of the Buddha: A Reader*, ed. Lucien Stryk, p. 159 et seq.

‡Cf. *Compassion in Tibetan Buddhism* by Tsong-ka-pa, ed. and trans. Jeffrey Hopkins, pp. 102-9.

more arduous, is infinitely more wondrous, for it is distinguished by the noble ideal of the Tathāgatas, the succession of compassionate ones who have "thus gone and thus come." Such was Bodhisattva-Gautama, who refused the nirvana of complete and perfect wisdom in order to live and work among the people and thus give another turn to the Wheel of the Law (Dharma). "What reason should I have to continually manifest myself?" — unless with the intent to awaken responsive souls to active participation in the ancient quest. The Buddha continues:

> When men become unbelieving, unwise, ignorant, careless, fond of sensual pleasures, and from thoughtlessness run into misfortune,
> Then I, who know the course of the world, declare: I am so and so [Tathāgata], (and consider): How can I incline them to enlightenment? how can they become partakers of the Buddha-laws (*buddhadharmāṇa*)?*

Buddhist texts tell of a series of Buddhas, the seventh of which was Gautama, whose ministry of 45 years was the culmination of choices made consistently over many lives for the "weal of gods and men," animals, and of all living beings. In his latest incarnation as Prince Siddhārtha his father, the king, had shielded him from everything that was ugly and painful. But at age 29 the call to seek the truth of things on his own account could not be suppressed. According to one legend, Gautama in disguise left the palace with his charioteer and on three successive nights was exposed to three "awakening sights": an old man, a leper,

---

*Saddharma-puṇḍarīka (The Lotus of the True Law), xv, §§22–3, trans. H. Kern, Sacred Books of the East 21:310.

and a corpse; and finally, a recluse, one who had renounced the world. He was profoundly shaken. A deep compassion filled his being; he would seek out the cause and cure of human sorrow. He left home, a beautiful wife and infant son, and all material comforts for begging bowl and monk's robe. For six years he experimented unwisely, undergoing the most stringent austerities until, near death from weakness and starvation, his inner voice told him that this was not the pathway to truth, that maltreating the body would avail nothing. Henceforth he would follow a middle course between extremes.

At length, after many tests of his resolve, on a full moon night of May he vowed not to move until he had attained *bodhi*, "wisdom, enlightenment." Sitting under a tree — since called the Bo or Bodhi tree — he withdrew into the inmost essence of his being. Māra, personification of destruction, tried repeatedly to deflect him, but Gautama was resolute and repelled every attack. When the moment of supreme illumination would be his, Māra summoned his minions for a tremendous final onslaught, but Gautama remained unmoved. Triumphant, he was *buddha*, "enlightened."

For 49 days he enjoyed the fullness of emancipation: omniscience and utter bliss were his for the taking. But instead of entering nirvana, his heart looked back upon sorrowing humankind and, perceiving with clarity the cause of man's confusion and the way to dispel it, he knew he must return. He would teach the Four Noble Truths and the Exalted Eightfold Path. Then a fleeting doubt entered his soul. Why give these priceless truths, so hard won, to a humanity that will pay scant heed? What purpose would be served?

The story runs that Brahmā, Lord and Creator of the universe, shot a thought into Gautama's brain: The world will be altogether lost if Bodhisattva-Tathāgata decides not to impart the *dharma* to man. Be compassionate to those who struggle; have mercy on those in the net of sorrow. If only a few will listen, the sacrifice will not be in vain. Then did Gautama after his lonely vigil mingle among the people and begin his ministry. And what was his message? When death was near, he summed up his life's purpose:

> O Ānanda, be ye lamps unto yourselves.* Be ye a refuge to yourselves. Betake yourselves to no external refuge. Hold fast to the truth as a lamp. Hold fast as a refuge to the truth. Look not for refuge to any one besides yourselves.†

Buddha's life and teaching, as recorded in legend and fact, are a sublime witness to the compassionate path. His plea — to love all beings and have a care for the well-being of animals as well as for our fellow humans, be diligent and eager to learn, mindful of thought and word — is as relevant in our time as it was 2,500 years ago when he discoursed on these themes with the brethren as they walked from village to village.

Many today are seriously striving to live by these precepts, while many others are asking: can knowledge of a

---

*The Pāli text is terse *attadīpa attasaraṇa* — *atta* (Sanskrit *ātman*) meaning "self," *dīpa*, "lantern," "light"; *saraṇa* (Skt: *śaraṇa*), "refuge."

†*Mahā-Parinibbāna-Sutta*, ii, §33, trans. T. W. Rhys Davids; Sacred Books of the East 11:38.

Buddha's renunciation or a Christ's sacrifice really transform human nature and effectively change a world situation which grows more parlous with every decade? We believe it can, though not immediately. Where *will* energizes the heart's intent, nothing is impossible. The very process of deep reflection on what the coming to earth of a Christ or a Buddha can mean to an aspiring soul, indeed to all humanity, exerts a refining and purifying influence on all facets of one's nature.

What is more, we can identify with Gautama because enlightenment was not conferred upon him; he *earned* his buddha-stature step by step over many lives. Yet even in this latest incarnation, after he had determined to penetrate the hidden causes of suffering and death, it took him several years of trial and error before he learned, almost at the cost of life, that the "middle way" is best; that nature has provided us with a marvelously tuned physical instrument which, if cared for and respected, may serve as the means of doing great good.

In a profound sense the path of compassion, of renunciation, is a path of sorrow because it means living in and for the world when one has long ago finished with the trials of earth life. Still a bodhisattva returns, impelled partly by karma and partly out of a deep love for his fellow humans. To each of us the choice is given, whether to advance for ourself and at last slip into the ocean of infinite bliss, forgetful of the world, or whether, when illumination comes, to resolve: "I cannot keep this wisdom to myself; I must return and help my brothers who need what light I have. They are sorrow-filled, confused, crying in the wilderness with aching hearts, yearning for truth." All the great teachers have chosen this pathway. They have come back to teach, to remind us of our divine lineage and to reawaken memory of our inborn knowledge, so that we may meet our destiny with courage and hope. This "deathless" path appeals to the altruism in us, in contrast to the path "for oneself." To choose between spirit and matter is an ongoing necessity if we are to evolve; to choose between truth for oneself and truth for others is by far the greater challenge.

The resolve to follow the bodhisattva lead is not made casually or for this one life only, but for all futurity: the consummation of divine awakening is ages in the making. All during the long and uphill wayfaring the soul's intent deepens and matures — to touch, if fleetingly, every life-particle within the ambience of its love.

13

The Pāramitās

In *The Voice of the Silence* H. P. Blavatsky epitomizes the compassionate course as follows:

> To live to benefit mankind is the first step. To practise the six glorious virtues is the second. — p. 33

The six glorious virtues are the *pāramitās* the neophyte is required to master as he travels the path that leads to the highest initiatory experience. Following Mahāyāna Buddhist terminology, HPB presents these "transcendental virtues" or "perfections" in her *Voice* as the "golden keys" that open the portals to masterhood. Buddhist texts of both Northern and Southern Schools list them variously in number and order, and at times with a different selection of "virtues." The words chosen for this or that "virtue," their number, or how they are arranged are of minor importance; what counts is fidelity to the endeavor to transcend the limitations of the ordinary self.

What are these pāramitās? Of the seven listed in the *Voice*, the first one is *dāna*, "giving," concern for others, being altruistic in thought, speech, and act. The second is *śīla*, "ethics," the high morality expected of the earnest disciple; the third, *kshānti*, "patience," forbearance, endurance, is the kindly perception that others' failings are no worse and perhaps less severe than one's own.

As for the fourth pāramitā, *virāga*, "dispassion," non-attachment to the effects upon us of the ups and downs of life: how difficult we find this and yet, if in our deepest self we cherish the bodhisattva ideal, the cultivation of virāga by no means condones indifference to the plight of others. Rather, it demands a wise exercise of compassion. It is interesting that to our knowledge this pāramitā is not given in the usual Sanskrit or Pāli lists. That the *Voice* includes virāga has significance in that the fourth position is pivotal, midway in the series of seven. We are reminded here of the seven stages of the initiatory cycle, of which the first three are preparatory, consisting chiefly of instruction and interior discipline.* In the fourth initiation the neophyte must *become* that which he has learned about, that is, he must identify with the inner realms of himself and of nature. If successful, he may attempt the three higher degrees, leading to suffering the god within to take possession of his humanity.

To become equal-minded in every circumstance, in joy and pain, success and failure, is to have attained the calm of a *muni*, a "sage"; it is fully to identify with the truth that whereas all that is born carries within it the seed of its decline, the indwelling wonder, the imperishable spirit, as so eloquently chanted in the *Bhagavad-Gītā*, is deathless, unperturbed by the pairs of opposites. To achieve the stature of a sage may seem rather distant for us; however, when we give the practice of virāga a fair trial, what a release this affords from the burden of tension we needlessly inflict upon ourselves — and, alas, on others.

---

*Cf. *The Mystery Schools*, pp. 41–58.

The fifth pāramitā is *vīrya,* "vigor," courage, resolution; the will and energy to stand staunch for what is true, and as strenuously oppose what is false. One proficient in vīrya is indefatigable in thought and deed. With the sixth, *dhyāna,* "meditation," profound contemplation, emptying oneself of all that is less than the highest, comes a natural awakening of latent powers, to culminate eventually in oneness with the essence of Being.

Finally, the seventh, *prajñā,* "enlightenment, wisdom" — "the key to which makes of man a god, creating him a bodhisattva, son of the Dhyānis." We will have become "god from mortal," as the Orphic candidate describes this sacred moment of the seventh initiation when transcendence and immanence become *one.*

Full mastery of the pāramitās, however enumerated, is naturally a long-term process, yet diligently seeking to practice them has the merit of producing more immediate benefits without risk of short-circuiting the psyche. The very decision to begin has a transforming effect on our attitude and outlook, and also on our relationship with others. Could we assess our ordinary selves from the vantage point of our wiser self, we would realize that a subtle, inner awakening is steadily in process; too subtle for us to graph, but cumulative in its effect on our present and future karma. We do not have to be "advanced" spiritually before consciously making the daily choices that distinguish the bodhisattva path from the pratyeka path. As we faithfully try to live these pāramitās, not only will we be nearer to realization of the universal brotherhood we all long for, but we shall be following the way of the Compassionate Ones.

Along with the daily cultivation of the pāramitās, the seedlings of altruism must be watered by the rains of compassion, notwithstanding the karmic obstructions in the nature that tend to inertia. Tsong-kha-pa, the sage of Tibet, held that the reverent practice of compassion is "the most excellent cause of Buddhahood, bearing the nature of thoroughly protecting all vulnerable sentient beings bound in the prison of cyclic existence."* This is *amrita-yāna* or the "deathless path" in its pure interpretation. When eventually a disciple is born into "the lineage of the Tathāgatas," he experiences surpassing joy — and yet immeasurable sorrow because of the obtuseness of so large a portion of mankind.

The present is heavy with the karma of past sowings by us all, but we should not discount the sowings of creative goodwill that have been nurtured through many lifetimes. If the latter seem long in maturing, we recall that Prince Siddhārtha did not become Buddha all at once: as far in the past as "four immensities ago" he vowed to become bodhisattva for the sake of sorrowing mankind. For scores of consecutive lives thereafter he tended the plant of compassion until ultimately it came to "full ripeness" in his latest birth at Kapilavastu, India.

Let us take a leap back into the long, long ago — to the "moment" in eternity when Gautama felt the first stirring of love for all mankind and visioned what could and ought to be, not merely for himself but for all living beings. Then was the seed of bodhisattvahood quickened into life and, bursting seedpod, it sent down a tiny rootlet into the virgin

---

*Compassion in Tibetan Buddhism, p. 101.

soil of his awakening consciousness. He made an earnest resolve to become ripe in wisdom and magnanimous of heart. Projecting his vision far into the future, he wills to build a raft of the dharma that he might ferry numberless millions over the ocean of illusion and pain to the other shore of freedom and light.

Way back then the Buddha of history was an ordinary person, aspiring, yes, but also, like ourselves, with character weaknesses, karmic impediments from previous lives not yet resolved. We may presume that he stumbled now and then and had to retrieve lost ground, and also that his associates in any one life may have received mixed karmic impingements from his errors of judgment as well as from his victories over self. It is no routine matter to go counter to the general drift but, because his motive was selfless, his resolve served as a steadying influence — life after life, the bodhisattva ideal was his inspiration and guide. Assuredly his ultimate triumph and renunciation would have thrice blessed all whose karma he had affected during his long gestation from ordinary man to buddha.

Every life-spark is a bodhisattva, a christos, a god *in process of becoming*. Hui-neng of China, the humble servant in the temple, understood this, and when his inner eye awakened and he became a Ch'an Buddhist master he put it this way:

> When not enlightened, buddhas are no other than ordinary beings; when there is enlightenment, ordinary beings at once turn into buddhas.*

---

*Cf. *The Sutra of Hui-neng*, trans. Thomas Cleary, p. 20.

The same possibility is ours: to begin now, in spite of the selfish and unruly traits that mar our nature, to sow the seeds of love and caring. Full enlightenment may be ages upon ages in the future, and although we too must make the supreme choice at the final moment of destiny, it will have been in the making all along the way. At each instant of our lives we are building into our character either the self-centeredness that eventually leads to pratyekahood, or the generosity of spirit that will impel us to take the first step on the bodhisattva path. Both paths are on the light side of nature, but there is, nonetheless, a clear distinction: as recorded in Buddhist writings, the pratyeka is compared to "the light of the moon" in contrast to the Tathāgata who "resembles the thousand-rayed disk of the autumnal sun."*

Every living being is the fruitage of a beginningless and endless outflowing from a divine seed, for within the seed-essence is the promise of what is to be: an immense potency, inert until the mystic moment when the life force bursts through and brings forth flower and fruit. Once a seed is sown in an appropriate environment, nature's elements of earth, water, air, and fire protect and stimulate its growth. So it is with ourselves: aided by the invisible counterparts of these elements, the seed-thoughts we sow daily and nightly leave their impress on the subtle energies coursing through our planet. Since we are one humanity, however separate at times we may feel ourselves to be, we share with all others what we *are*, our finest and our meanest. What a responsibility is ours, but also what a superb

---

*Buddhaghosa, quoted in *World of the Buddha*, p. 160.

opportunity. Just as we are sensitive to the lower strata of thought forces when we are despondent, just so may we resonate with the upper regions of earth's auric atmosphere and perchance hear, if we are quiet, the subtle whisperings that inspire to wonder and noble deeds.

Many today, in their dedicated labors to relieve the suffering of millions, are manifesting a quality of mercy which may have been fanned by a gesture of friendship and understanding made by some bodhisattva-to-be in lives past. Perhaps we too have been similarly moved. The thought is deeply humbling and makes one all the more resolved to follow the lead of the Enlightened Ones who are infinitely patient and perceptive. Small wonder a Buddha of Compassion returns to teach. He is impelled to do so by the karma of all whose destinies have intersected his in former cycles; even more is he impelled by a love so all-embracing it enfolds the entirety of nature's kingdoms, a love that fortifies new aspirants and those who possibly in a future life may experience the first intimations of concern for others' well-being.

The Buddhist Confession of Faith succinctly expresses the essence of Buddhist philosophy and practice:

> Buddhaṃ śaraṇaṃ gacchāmi
> Dharmaṃ śaraṇaṃ gacchāmi
> Saṅghaṃ śaraṇaṃ gacchāmi
>
> I go to buddha for refuge
> I go to dharma for refuge
> I go to the assembly (devotees, followers) for refuge

We place our trust in Buddha as the imbodiment of the

"Great Sacrifice," the supreme initiator and protector of humanity, who makes it possible for avatāras and bodhisattvas periodically to illumine the fields of human consciousness.

We place our trust in dharma, in the primal truths that enlighten us on universal nature and the soul, identifying with which we glimpse our cosmic purpose.

We place our trust in saṅgha, the brotherhood or company of seekers, a fellowship which includes the entirety of the human life-wave.

In placing trust and loyalty in one another as brother aspirants, we share in a companionship that links us magnetically with the spiritual heart of our planet, the Brotherhood of Adepts. Insofar as we give allegiance to their purposes, we are partners in this universal fraternity which is dedicated to lifting — as far as world karma will permit — the burden of sorrow and misery and ignorance that is the scourge of humanity. If enough men and women will not only believe in, but also follow their intuitions and consciously cast their lot with the cause of compassion, there is every reason to have confidence that our civilization will one day make the leap from self-centeredness to genuine brotherhood in every phase of the human enterprise.

To quicken in aspiring human hearts the ancient vow to light their lamps from the flame of compassion is the noblest and the most beautiful ideal, and one which, if steadfastly held, gives stimulus and depth to aspiration.

H. P. Blavatsky and The Theosophical Society

IN 1888 THE PUBLICATION OF *The Secret Doctrine* by HPB challenged the accepted dicta of theologians and scientists, and markedly redirected the thinking of the twentieth century. Hers was a worldview that reckoned the life cycles of galaxies and atoms as part of the same evolutionary process that returns the human soul again and again to earth life.

Who was HPB and what is The Theosophical Society she helped to found? Helena Petrovna Blavatsky (née von Hahn) was born in the Ukraine at Ekaterinoslav (Dnepropetrovsk) on the river Dnieper on August 12, 1831 (July 31, Old Style Russian calendar). Her father, Captain of Artillery Peter Alexeyevich von Hahn, was a descendant of the Counts Hahn von Rottenstern-Hahn, an old Mecklenburg family from Germany, and her mother, Helena Andreyevna, daughter of Privy Councillor A. M. de Fadeyev and Princess Helena Pavlovna Dolgorukova, was a gifted novelist who spoke out against oppression, particularly of women. She suffered from ill health most of her short life, and died at age 29. Helena, then eleven, with her sister Vera and infant brother Leonid, left Odessa to live with their maternal grandparents, the de Fadeyevs, at Saratov, and later at Tiflis in the Caucasus.

Mme. de Fadeyev was a woman of rare wisdom and scholastic attainment, a botanist respected throughout Europe, versed in history and the natural sciences, including archaeology. Her unusual endowments of mind and spirit, plus an extensive library at the Fadeyev home, nurtured and fortified Helena's determination to find truth for herself, whatever the risk. Married in 1849 in name only to Nikifor Blavatsky, a man more than twice her age, Helena ran away after three months, gaining the freedom she longed for. Then began years of seemingly restless wanderings and travels over the globe, encounters with the wise and the less wise on every continent. Avidly she sought the Ariadne thread that would lead her to those teachers and life experiences that would sharpen her intuition and enlarge her compassion.*

During this period HPB was being trained and prepared to lead a spiritual movement that would shake the tree of orthodoxy to its roots, and at the same time direct public attention to the fruits of the *tree of life* that could be won by all sincere seekers willing and ready to undergo the required discipline.

HPB was in Paris in 1873 when her teachers ordered her to go to America and begin her work. She left immediately and arrived in New York City on July 7. In October of the following year she met Henry Steel Olcott who had been

---

*See *HPB: The Extraordinary Life and Influence of Helena Blavatsky* by Sylvia Cranston, 3rd rev. ed.; *H. P. Blavatsky and the Theosophical Movement* by Charles J. Ryan, 2nd rev. ed.; H. P. Blavatsky, *Collected Writings,* 1874–1878, ed. Boris de Zirkoff, 1:xxv–lii; and *H. P. Blavatsky, Tibet and Tulku* by Geoffrey A. Barborka, pp. 6–41.

H. P. Blavatsky and The Theosophical Society / 147

sent by the *Daily Graphic* to the Eddy homestead in Vermont to investigate the phenomena that were reportedly happening there. The two of them were to work closely together in the formation and development of The Theosophical Society.

Exactly two years after coming to America, HPB received further orders, as she noted in the first of her "Scrap Books":

> *Orders* received from India direct to establish a philosophico-religious Society & choose a name for it — also to choose Olcott. July 1875.*

So it was that on September 7, 1875, at her residence in New York City, HPB hosted a small group of spiritualists, kabbalists, physicians, and lawyers — all of them fascinated by the "occult" or hidden side of nature — to hear a lecture by George Henry Felt on "The Lost Canon of Proportion of the Egyptians." During the course of the evening, the idea of forming a Society for this kind of study was proposed. The sixteen or so desirous of joining met the following and subsequent evenings to formalize their intent. By October 30th a Preamble and Bylaws had been agreed upon and printed, with the objects of the Society, "to collect and diffuse a knowledge of the laws which govern the universe." On November 17, 1875, an Inaugural Meeting at Mott Memorial Hall in New York City launched The Theosophical Society with an address by its President-Founder, Henry S. Olcott. The name "theosophy" had been adopted be-

---

*The Golden Book of The Theosophical Society: 1875–1925, p. 19; H. P. Blavatsky, *Collected Writings* 1:94.

cause it best described that philosophico-religious system which conceives of the Divine as emanating itself in a series of progressions, and also recognizes the human soul as being capable of attaining mystical and spiritual illumination. The brotherhood ideal was not explicitly stated, but was implicit in the Preamble which affirmed that membership was open to all, regardless of race, gender, or creed.

In 1875 The Theosophical Society was a completely unknown venture. No one realized, except perhaps those who were behind the Movement, what the long-range effect would be of that small handful who dared to form a body that would seriously investigate the inner laws that move and sustain the outer physical universe. While the reception given to her teachings was remarkable for that era, HPB had nonetheless to face strong opposition among scholars, scientists, and theologians, not to mention the popular press. To many she was an iconoclast of a stature they could not comprehend — here was a woman of fearless purpose, toppling every sacred cow, not only in her large two-volume work, *Isis Unveiled* (1877), but also in a spate of newspaper and magazine articles. They couldn't believe that she wasn't out to destroy the living message of the world's religious teachers or the proven facts of science. On the contrary, her purpose was simple and direct: to inveigh against everything of a dead-letter and hypocritical nature, while opening wide the windows of closed minds to the invigorating breezes of independent thought and a philosophy of cosmic dimension.

To better appreciate who Helena Blavatsky was, we must view her as the bearer of a message, spokesman for those wiser than she, members of a brotherhood of guardians and protectors of humanity who hold in trust the truths about man's spiritual origin and destiny — truths which are given out when the call from the hearts of men and women is importunate enough to draw forth a further unveiling of nature's hidden lore. Prior to 1875 the Western world was scarcely aware that advanced human beings existed, despite the fact that in India, Tibet, China, and the Near East, legend and scripture testify to an association of sages who from time to time send out one of their number to live and work among this or that people. To become worthy to be taken in hand by a guru or teacher was held as the highest spiritual boon, and many an aspirant for chelaship would strive for years, without any sign of recognition, to prepare himself by purification and self-abnegation to be accepted for training. All of this was typically Eastern in atmosphere and practice.

Then, with the coming of HPB to America, everything changed. The cycle was evidently ripe for the Mahatmas (variously called Adepts, Masters, or the Brothers) to make themselves and their spiritualizing work for humanity more generally understood. The Theosophical Society was inspired by two Mahatmas whose chiefs had searched the globe for nearly a century before finding one who could be trained to receive and transmit the teaching; and, what is more, who could and would willingly bear the karma of enlightening a world heavily steeped in pride of material accomplishment.* These two, later known as M and KH,

---

*See *The Mahatma Letters to A. P. Sinnett*, Letter XXVI, p. 203.

went to their Chief and said: Let us try and see if we cannot bring about a center of effort and inspire a few individuals who will work for the enlightenment of mankind. The Chief was doubtful, but agreed to let them try. They did not look for perfect people. Had they waited until HPB, Olcott, Judge, and others who wanted to help had become perfect, The Theosophical Society might never have been born. The wonder of it is that those early theosophists had the courage to support an ideal that was seemingly beyond realization: to establish a nucleus of men and women who would give their finest energies to furthering the ideal of universal brotherhood.

Almost immediately after public disclosure of their existence, Masters and Adepts, under various initials and names, became the talk of theosophists and their contemporaries. Inevitably, people with little or no knowledge of what discipleship entails wanted personal contact with the Brothers. For many, this was a natural and spontaneous outpouring of love and esteem for those great beings who imbodied all that they aspired to be. Some, no doubt, simply wanted to be special. Others reacted with scorn and ridicule; little did they realize what profound compassion moved these friends of mankind. HPB came to regret that she had ever allowed "phenomena and the *Masters*" to become public knowledge (*Blavatsky Letters*, p. 97). After a relatively few years, the Masters withdrew from outer contact with the Society, yet retained the link inwardly with HPB and with the heart of the Movement, to remain the guiding inspiration of subsequent generations of seekers.

Today the subject of Mahatmas and their direct or indirect influence on individuals or groups, and on humanity as a whole, is again to the fore. Many theosophists prefer to say as little as possible about Masters and about Śambhala, in order not to desecrate further what is inexpressibly sacred, although they clearly acknowledge HPB and her teachers as the source of theosophy and its ideals.

Assuredly the Masters are behind every truly unselfish effort to lift the burden of sorrow and ignorance from mankind, and the theosophical movement is not the Brotherhood's only source of "building stones." "The sun of Theosophy must shine for all, not for a part," wrote M to A. P. Sinnett early in 1882. "There is more of this movement than you have yet had an inkling of, and the work of the T.S. is linked in with similar work that is secretly going on in all parts of the world. . . . You know K.H. and me — buss! know you anything of the *whole* Brotherhood and its ramifications?" And M reminds Sinnett that he "ought to have learned by this time our ways. We *advise* — and never *order*. But we *do* influence individuals."* It is not for us to put enclosures around the Masters even in thought and, whether consciously or unconsciously, try to decree what their work is and what it is not, and how or whom they will inspire or influence. Equally must we be careful not to prejudge anyone and automatically dub him a pretender because he professes to be the "mouthpiece of Mahatmas," or to receive "messages" from Morya, Koothoomi, or Djual Khool.

We should not be astonished at the proliferation of al-

**The Mahatma Letters*, Letter XLVII, pp. 271–2.

leged gurus, avatars, ascended masters, reincarnations of HPB, swamis, and messengers. A number of people have taken the Masters' teachings and created from them a fantasy of psychic imagination, a travesty of theosophy. Yet it seems incredible, with the publication of the original letters of the Mahatmas to A. P. Sinnett and others, now readily available in libraries and bookstores, that so much notice is taken of counterfeit mahatmas and messengers who trade on the anxieties of the times and the vulnerability of the innocent whose very sincerity makes them easy prey. It would be farcical were it not so tragic, with lives scarred by the betrayal.

At the same time, neither the Masters and their letters, nor *The Secret Doctrine* or any of HPB's writings, are the basis of a creed or "bible." The Theosophical Society has no articles of belief, no dogmas; freedom of inquiry, of aspiration, of self-evolution, is its watchword. HPB made it clear over and over again that what she was bringing was a portion only of the eternal wisdom-religion; that she was a transmitter of that which she had received. Through her titanic genius she gave it forth in the best way she could, but she didn't claim that every word was sacrosanct. She laid these truths before us, saying, after Montaigne, "I have . . . brought nothing of my own but the string that ties them" — cut the string up, if you will, but you cannot destroy truth.*

Inevitably HPB had many detractors. For example, in 1885 the Society for Psychical Research (SPR) published a

---

*Cf. *The Secret Doctrine* 1:xlvi.

report by Richard Hodgson, stating that HPB had written the letters from the Mahatmas* herself, and the SPR concluded that HPB was "one of the most accomplished, ingenious, and interesting impostors in history."† Over the years friends and supporters of HPB had time and again sought a retraction, but to little avail. Then in 1986, "impelled by a strong feeling of the need for JUSTICE," Vernon Harrison, Ph.D., handwriting expert and longtime member of the SPR, published a critique of the Hodgson Report titled: "J'Accuse: An Examination of the Hodgson Report of 1885," followed in 1997 by "J'Accuse d'autant plus [I accuse all the more]: A Further Study of the Hodgson Report." Over a period of some fifteen years, Dr. Harrison had made an exhaustive study of the handwritings of the Mahatmas' letters and found the Hodgson Report to be "badly flawed and untrustworthy" and that there was "no evidence of common origin between the 'KH', 'M', and 'HPB' scripts."‡ Yet in spite of the attacks on her character by Hodgson and others, HPB continued to write what was to become *The Secret Doctrine.*

In 1886 HPB issued a powerful statement in which she clarifies what the original program of The Theosophical

---

*This collection of holographic letters was presented in 1939 by Sinnett's executrix, Maud Hoffman, to the British Museum (now British Library) where they can be viewed by the public.

†Cf. *Proceedings of The Society for Psychical Research*, London, England, Part IX, December 1885, pp. 201–400.

‡Dr. Harrison's critiques have been issued in one volume with 13 full color plates under the title: *H. P. Blavatsky and the SPR: An Examination of the Hodgson Report of 1885*, Theosophical University Press, 1997.

Society was and remains today. Therein she says that the founders "had to oppose in the strongest manner possible anything approaching *dogmatic faith and fanaticism* — belief in the *infallibility* of the Masters, or even in the very existence of our invisible Teachers, having to be checked from the first."* She and Olcott weren't told what to do, but they were distinctly told what *not* to do; in particular, they should never permit The Theosophical Society to become a sect: dogmatic in thought and dogmatic in deed. The strength of theosophy is that there is no teaching that anyone has to believe before he can participate actively as a member or supporter of The Theosophical Society. The one requirement is that he accept the principle of universal brotherhood as of great validity and a power in his thinking and acting. He may remain a Buddhist, a Christian, a Zoroastrian, an atheist, or whatever: "The greatest spirit of free research untrammeled by anyone or anything, had to be encouraged."†

This original program is imbodied in the objectives of The Theosophical Society which, however worded, remain in principle as follows: to diffuse among men a knowledge of the laws inherent in the universe; to promulgate the knowledge of the essential unity of all that is, and to demonstrate that this unity is fundamental in nature; to form an active brotherhood among men; to encourage the study of ancient and modern religion, science, and philosophy; and, to investigate the powers innate in man.

---

*The Original Programme of The Theosophical Society, p. 6; reprint, H. P. Blavatsky, *Collected Writings* 7:148.
†Ibid.

A study of the religious and philosophical scriptures releases a flood of ideas because, when we look into the sacred writings of world civilizations from the expanded perspective that theosophy provides, we discern the one universal wisdom expressed in many forms. Familiarity with the traditions and scriptures of earlier peoples also helps us maintain a sense of proportion. We come to appreciate that this grand universal system of truths is the common inheritance of mankind, but that periodically it finds a "unique" expression in order to meet the specific needs of a given era. This explains why this or that nation or race believes itself to be the "chosen people" — it is because at a certain historic period they *were* chosen by the messenger of the time to receive a new light, a new directive for spiritual living.

Note the careful wording of the last objective: the phrase used is "to investigate the powers innate in man," not to *develop* psychic powers. There is a wide difference. We are encouraged to understand ourselves as multifold beings, to study and inquire into the full range of our human potentialities. However, there is a tacit warning here against unnaturally developing powers that could lead to an overemphasis of the psychic and astral aspects of our constitution at the expense of our intuitive and spiritual faculties. HPB came bitterly to regret that she had shown a few trusted ones certain feats of phenomenal power in the hope of demonstrating that there was a world of subtle forces back of the physical one. Today many would like to have such extranormal powers, but how many can honestly say they want to cultivate them from utterly selfless motives? After all, what intrinsic value do these powers have? It is well to examine our motive, to be certain it is truly selfless. We all have too much selfishness in our *spiritual* desires as well as in our material natures, and selfishness in the higher principles is far more tenacious than in the lower nature where it is comparatively easy to overcome.

The theosophic purpose, then, is manifold, and no one was more aware than H. P. Blavatsky of the magnitude of the task before her. She lived and worked in the tradition of those who labor ceaselessly to awaken humanity to its innate grandeur. "By their fruits shall ye know them." With every decade she is becoming more widely accepted as an opener of the gateways of the soul. By her retelling of the archaic wisdom-teachings she revealed the inspired source of the many traditions and scriptures of mankind, and unfolded the wondrous drama of the genesis and evolution of worlds and of man. To many her greatest gift was her pointing once again to the "path," the sacred way of inner mastery — not for oneself, but for the uplifting of all beings everywhere. Her lasting appeal to men and women of compassion is to work actively for the realization of universal brotherhood so that eventually every people, nation, and race will be free to pursue its individual destiny in harmony and at peace with all others.

15

Who Will Save Us?

THE TWENTIETH CENTURY WITNESSED unspeakable tyrannies of soul and body. It is as though an Armageddon were in process before our eyes, between the altruistic urgings of the heart and the selfish demands of the personal nature, between the creative energies and the destructive, the spiritual and the psychic/material. As evolving beings we either progress or retrogress, there is no standing still; since every moment we are either creators or destroyers, it is essential that periodically we are shocked into a deeper awareness of our divine purpose.

Ideas are more potent than spears or bombs for shaking us out of our lethargy, and what could have been more revolutionary than the revival of ideas long forgotten: of universal brotherhood, of the *oneness* of all life, of divinity rather than matter as the kinetic agency behind evolution? It is these ideas, injected into the thought-consciousness of humanity in the nineteenth century, that slowly and steadily germinated during the twentieth century with mixed results: on the one hand, arousing a fury of reaction from entrenched establishments and, on the other, finding response in the aspirations of earnest men and women of every age and background.

The awful uncertainties of the times are a blessing, in that they impel us to reexamine our thinking and motives and to come to terms with the central issues of life and death, and how best to prepare our children for the world they are inheriting. Science with its "miraculous pitcher" of marvels has confirmed our interdependence not only as a humanity but, more importantly, as participants in an ecosphere whose families of entities share in the one life flow. Yet with all our knowledge we have not discovered what we most need: how to live in harmony with ourselves and with one another. As a result, many are despondent, fearful of themselves and of the future, seriously questioning where civilization is heading.

It should not surprise us that various Fundamentalists are urging us to "believe and be saved" before it is too late: for the "perilous times" of which both Paul and Peter wrote are soon to come, when the corrupt and the covetous, the truce-breakers and despisers of all that is good, will walk the land, "the heavens will pass away with great noise, and the elements melt with fervent heat, the earth also . . ."* We would do well not to wholly discount such warnings, for no species can escape the consequences of action; certainly not we humans, who should know better than wantonly to violate natural law. Of course, since every living being in the universe is subject to birth and death, and rebirth in a new form, so likewise our present civilization, and our planet and its kingdoms of lives, will eventually disappear after fulfilling their respective life cycles.

---

*Cf. *2 Timothy* 3:1–5 and *2 Peter* 3:3–13.

The destruction of earth and the retreat of the gods as the human race becomes increasingly matter-bound is a recurring theme in ancient cultures. The narratives vary in externals: in one instance they might refer to an age and a people that have long since vanished or to predictions of what has not yet come to pass. At first blush, the accounts of the cataclysmic destruction of everything are terrifying — whether we ponder the cryptic verses of Nostradamus (1503–1566), the *Book of Revelation*, or other apocalyptic writings. But when we read further in the world's sacred literatures, we discover that the dying of the old cycle is followed in time by the emergence of the new: earth comes forth fresh and without blemish, and a new humanity arises. This is poetically foretold in the Icelandic *Edda*, in the prophecy of Vala, the Sibyl, who forecasts the coming of *Ragnarök* ("doom or return of gods"), with "sun growing dim, earth sinking, and stars falling," accompanied by fire rising high to complete the desolation.* At length, another earth rises from the waters, the eagle flies, and gods again decree peace in the land and what is to be held sacred.

A like pattern of decline, death, and renewal is seen in the discourse among Asclepius and his friends, attributed to Hermes Trismegistus, the "thrice-greatest." When in the course of time "all things hostile to the nature of the soul" have been committed by mankind, earth will "no longer stand unshaken, . . . heaven will not support the stars in their orbits, . . . all voices of the gods will of necessity be silenced. . . . But when all this has befallen, Asclepius,

---

*Cf. *The Masks of Odin* by Elsa-Brita Titchenell, "Völuspá" (The Sibyl's Prophecy), pp. 87–100.

then the Master and Father, God, the first before all . . . will stay the disorder by the counterworking of his will." He will call back to the path all who have strayed, cleanse the earth of evil, now with flood, now with fire, or again, "expelling it by war and pestilence." Then in the process of ages will "God, the maker and restorer of the mighty fabric," make way for "the new birth of the Kosmos . . . a holy and awe-striking restoration of all nature."*

The *Vishṇu-Purāṇa* of ancient India graphically portrays the decline and renewal of humanity and the earth. After detailing the iniquities of mankind "until the human race approaches its annihilation" toward the close of *kali yuga,* our present age, it foretells the renovation that will occur when "a portion of that divine being who exists, of his own spiritual nature, in the character of Brahma, and who is the beginning and the end, and who comprehends all things, shall descend upon earth." This is Kalki, the tenth avatāra or divine incarnation, who will be born in the village of Śambhala to destroy all that is false and unrighteous, and reestablish dharma, the law of truth, purity, and duty. Those whose minds will be awakened and changed by virtue of that remarkable period "shall be as the seeds of human beings, and shall give birth to a race who shall follow the laws of the *Kṛita* age (or age of purity)," known also as *satya yuga* (age of truth).†

According to Brahmanical records kali yuga — lowest of the four ages, and with a life span of 432,000 years — began in 3102 BC upon the death of Krishna, the eighth

---

**Hermetica, trans. Walter Scott, 1:344–7, "Asclepius — III," §26a.
† *The Vishṇu Purāṇa*, trans. H. H. Wilson, 4:224–9, bk. 4, ch. 24.

avatāra of Vishnu. Presuming that these time cycles are reasonably accurate, this means we have completed only a little more than 5,000 years of kali yuga, with some 427,000 years yet to run! Moreover, as kali yuga is held to contain but one-quarter of *satya* or truth in contrast to the four-quarters of truth present in the kṛita age, it looks as though humanity is on a downslide — a most discouraging prospect unless we view our present age within the larger context of the evolutionary cycle of earth. The crucial factor here is that earth and its inhabitants have progressed beyond the halfway point in their evolution; they have completed their downward thrust and, having passed the nadir, if only slightly, have begun the climb upward out of matter toward an ever more refined spirituality. Thus, kali yuga is a minor cycle of descent within a larger cycle of ascent on which we and earth have embarked; in fact, even during our present kali age there occur periods of relative spirituality.

In a letter to Allan O. Hume written in 1882, HPB's mentor KH explains that when humanity passes the "*axial point*," the midpoint in its septenary course, "the world teems with the results of intellectual activity and *spiritual decrease*"; and that it is in the latter half of the long evolutionary arc that "the spiritual Ego will begin its real struggle with body and mind to manifest its transcendental powers." He closes his long letter by asking: "Who will help in the forthcoming gigantic struggle? Who? Happy the man who helps a helping hand."* Who, indeed, will lend a helping hand in this contest of ages?

The Mahatma Letters, Letter XIV, p. 88.

Many today are longing for a savior to put to rout the destroyers and restore harmony and brotherly love among us. As far back in time as legend and scripture record, practically every people has cherished the promise of a Redeemer at the end of the dark age who is to vanquish the evildoers and lead the blameless to an earth made new, a golden age when truth is honored and all life held sacred. The Christian looks to the Second Coming when the ultimate winnowing will occur; orthodox Jewry awaits the Messiah; Parsis count upon Saoshyans to overthrow Ahriman (darkness) and enthrone Ahura Mazda (light). In India similar apocalyptic events surround the avatāra Kalki at the close of kali yuga; Buddhist writings describe a future Buddha, Maitreya, the "Friendly, Benevolent One," leaving the celestial regions for earth in order once again to impart the Dharma (the sacred Law) in its purity; and Tibetan legends tell of the return of the Kings of Śambhala. No two agree on the timing: Oriental peoples placing the event far in the future, while Westerners announce the coming of a Savior or World-Teacher to be practically upon us.

With our foreshortened view of human destiny, due in part to rejection of reincarnation as a valid philosophical hypothesis, it is no surprise that recent decades have seen a rise in the West of a kind of messianism, manifesting in a hysterical longing for some enlightened Personage to rise up and pull our civilization back from self-annihilation.

That teachers and guides are as necessary to our inner development as are loving parents and schoolteachers for children is self-evident, but the other half of the equation is equally relevant. Just as the growing child must be allowed to find his or her own strength, so humanity as a whole needs time and space to reach maturity through its own efforts. We are much like the adolescent who rejects the help that is available and then, feeling alienated, seeks foolish and sometimes destructive means to fill the loneliness. In consequence, while there is currently an extraordinary yearning for higher guidance, there is also an astonishing lack of discrimination as to what is sound and what is spurious in matters of the spirit.

Today, the winds of Nārada, agent of karma, are toppling once seemingly impregnable barriers to make way for long-needed changes in individual and national destinies.* Every nation, race, and people, indeed every human being over the globe, is subject to the bipolar force of Nārada's Śiva-energy which destroys that it may rebuild. Upheavals of lesser and greater magnitude occur cyclically to insure the viability of spirit through shedding and renewal of forms. This interplay between light and shadow will continue as long as we are imbodied entities. But there are cycles within cycles, and the growth patterns of humanity reveal long periods of seeming quiescence, punctuated by apparently sudden changes. When such a "moment" of destiny has matured, we may have an influx of a new type of humanity on the scene, often accompanied by global disturbances of a physical as well as psychological character.

In minor degree the waning of the Piscean and the dawning of the Aquarian age is such a nodal point, where the struggle between the old and the new is joined. As we

---

*Cf. G. de Purucker, *Fountain-Source of Occultism*, pp. 689-95.

are at the intersection of two major astronomical cycles and, possibly, of still longer ones as well, we wonder whether the convergence of these several cycles produces unusually strong "tidal" effects that could allow a huge wave of egos to seek incarnation at this time. Whether the incoming tide brings a resurgence of spiritual values, or an even darker period of human suffering, will depend largely upon the present and coming generations. We humans, individually and collectively as planetary citizens, are being impelled to wake up and reexamine our thinking and behavior; many are turning inward for answers, questioning motives and the why and how of existence.

Wherever we look, we observe the forces of progress and of retrogression vying for dominion of minds and souls. When viewed in isolation this is cause for real concern, but when seen as symptomatic of a much needed harrowing process, we have grounds for hope that the new seeding will germinate in fertile soil. Just as cyclic renewal of forms occurs in every kingdom so that the new flowering can take place, so fresh and dynamic insights into the role and destiny of man and of our cosmic parent can rejuvenate our thought-structures.

For those who have touched the theosophic stream in former lives, but who as yet may be unaware of the responsibility this imposes, such could be the moment of awakening the higher self is waiting for — when once again we inwardly connect up with ourselves and resume the unending quest. From then on our lives take on a new dimension: no longer content to drift, the inner struggle intensifies between our Ariadne self which would lead us out of the maze of material interests, and our personal self which for a time tries to ignore its guidance. But our Ariadne will never let us quite forget — it cannot, for we are bound to it irrevocably. It is none other than our *sūtrātman,* the "thread of radiance" that unites us to our god-self. More wondrous still, it also links us to the god-self or ātman of every human being who has ever lived on earth — a cosmic oneness that is beyond the power of man, god, or demon to annihilate.

Not everyone, however, is able to respond constructively to the tumult of change. Many are baffled and, as a result, veer between the secure dogmas of the past and every avant-garde notion that captures their fancy. Where is the saving middle way that will steadily enhance the transmutation process from dependence on external guidance to reliance on the savior within?

It would be a pitiless universe had humanity to wait many thousands of years for the golden age to return before receiving help. Could we see our human evolution from the origins of this earth cycle as in a panorama, we would know that a hierarchy of Compassionate Ones keeps a protective watch over all of earth's children. Aside from their cyclical seeding of the world consciousness with as much of cosmic truth as humanity's karma will permit, periodically they send one or more of their number to incarnate among mankind and enjoin nations and races to live in harmony, order, and peace one with another. To establish a universal brotherhood on earth is their continuing dream. Nor is it an impossible dream by virtue of our common origin in divinity — on this basis we *are* brothers.

By the law of magnetic attraction, when the call from

awakening minds and hearts is powerful enough a response is forthcoming. "Ask, and it shall be given you . . ." But before "asking" too earnestly — wishes do have an uncomfortable way of coming true — perhaps we should ask ourselves some questions: Do we merit the help we seek? Have we done all we can and should do to right the wrongs in our own natures and in the larger arena of world relationships? Further, is our intuition sensitive enough to recognize a true messenger or teacher? Conversely, what certainty is there that a person is what he claims to be, and that his teachings accord with nature and with the primeval truths impressed upon our inmost essence when humanity was young? False prophets are ever present, while those who are genuine often are maligned; it may be only after one of them has left the earth scene that we intuit a great soul has lived among us. Surely a high degree of perception, purity of aspiration, and plain common sense are required.

Out-and-out charlatans represent no lasting threat, for they are spotted fairly soon. It is charismatic figures with their persuasive medley of half-truths who pose the greatest test for their followers — and for themselves. Many of them probably start out with good intent, to bring a message of hope to the millions who are hungering for something more than the tight orthodoxy of credal faiths. A few of them, perhaps after some peak experience or vision, are convinced they have received a "call." This may or may not be the case. Where aspiration is strong and one-pointed, an individual may for an instant open a channel to the light within and undergo a temporary fusion of soul with his higher self. For him the vision is real. The question is: Has there been a corresponding purification of character, a parallel disciplining and control of the passional and mental nature to sustain the vision? Unless he has ruthlessly striven to denude himself of self-pride and greed, the momentary opening to the inner worlds leaves him vulnerable to alien forces from the lower astral realms which, when not controlled by the higher will, may turn demonic.

We recall an astute observation made by William Law (1686–1761), theosopher, Christian divine, and a profound student of the writings of Jakob Boehme:

> Would you know . . . whence it is, that so many false Spirits have appeared in the World, who have deceived themselves and others with false Fire, and false Light, laying Claim to Inspirations, Illuminations, and Openings of the Divine Life, pretending to do Wonders under extraordinary Calls from God? It is this; they have turned to God without turning from themselves; would be alive in God, before they were dead to their own Nature . . .
>
> Now Religion in the Hands of Self, or corrupt Nature, serves only to discover Vices of a worse kind, than in Nature left to itself.*

Note the phrase: "they have turned to God without turning from themselves." Human nature hasn't changed much over the centuries! How many of those, eager for transformative experiences of a higher order, are willing to take the first steps in self-discipline, much less endure long and arduous training and testing of integrity and motive over life-

---

*William Law, *The Spirit of Prayer: or The Soul Rising out of the Vanity of Time, into the Riches of Eternity*, Prayer 2.1–32; cf. Aldous Huxley, *The Perennial Philosophy*, p. 243.

times? "Discipline precedes the Mysteries" is an axiom of proven validity.

It has happened in historic times and is happening today that one or another self-proclaimed guru comes to believe that he is infallible: is he not God-sent, an apostle of the Messiah, or a bearer of messages direct from the Lord Maitreya? His or her followers are also culpable in part, for continuous and unthinking adulation can act as an intoxicant. So insidious is the poison of flattery that all too soon the would-be teacher convinces both himself and his devotees that he is absolved from the strict morality required of others: whatever transgression of the ethical code he may incur becomes a "holy act" and thus sanctified. There is no way to measure the tragic consequences of such betrayal — on himself and on those who unstintingly give of their devotion and trust.

Obviously, perfection is neither possible nor expected, and it is both presumptuous and unfair to judge harshly those who earnestly strive to give spiritual and moral aid to their fellow humans. Nevertheless, we have the right and duty to expect of those who profess to teach, that words of truth and compassion are authenticated by honorable and altruistic thinking and doing. What all of us need is a clearer knowledge of ourselves plus a healthy dose of skepticism — not cynicism, but intelligent skepticism. The word is apt, from the Greek *skeptikos*, "thoughtful, reflective." We need to be reminded that the essence of our being is immortal and that each of us has not only the inborn capacity and the will but also the obligation to "save" ourselves — that is, to liberate our souls from the fetters of selfish desire.

The cyclic appearance of savior figures is to remind us of our divine possibilities, not to deprive us of our urge to grow and become as they are. We can begin now by jettisoning from our nature all that is extraneous and less than we esteem in human behavior. There is no call for exaggerated physical or mental austerities: practice of the ancient and universally honored precepts — call them commandments, beatitudes, pāramitās, or virtues — is our open sesame to the future. In spite of the pull toward material concerns in kali yuga's descending cycle, we do not have to be downtending in our thinking or aspiration. The history of mankind from the earliest era confirms that in every age, whether one of spiritual clarity and upward reach or one of spiritual darkness and downward bent, pioneers are quietly at work, forward-thinking men and women who keep alive the fires of aspiration. The stronger the pull matterwards, the more powerfully they swim against it in order to produce the needed countercurrent.

Patently, we are in the midst of a critical period where the light energies are in direct contest with the dark forces — not only on the national and international scene, but within our own natures. Unless we begin now, individually and collectively, to rely on our own inner strength, we will have little to draw upon in future crises. This isn't the time to lean on great leaders; it isn't the time to wait for a messenger. If we feel that the odds are overwhelmingly against our steadfast efforts to hold aloft the torch of hope, let us recall Mother Teresa. When asked how she could bear up under the enormity of suffering she witnessed daily, without any possibility of her stemming the tide appreciably, she replied: "One and one and one: I look only at the child or the old man or woman I am tending; if I thought of the millions and millions who need my help I could do nothing."

It seems to me that every human being has within him the power to do what is required: privately and unnoticed to follow the lead of his higher self. But we have to persevere in this practice; above all, we have to trust unreservedly in the potency of our inner light to illumine our lives. If each one of us steadfastly heeds its guidance, in time we will become an imbodiment of compassion, understanding, knowledge, and helpfulness — and yet, paradoxically, we will have achieved the greatest boon of all, we will have become as "nothing in the eyes of the world." In this manner will we strengthen the light-impulses that are gaining in number and momentum, and by so much fortify the compassionate labors of those who work unceasingly for all nations and for the unborn and who are, even now, readying the way for the dawn of a brighter age.

16

The Daily Initiation

EVERY PEOPLE HAS BORNE the sacred burden of the Divine in its deepest heart. How strange, with this wondrous heritage, that we should ever feel "widowed of the presence of the gods," as though the link with our divine source had become frayed, no longer assured. We are not the first civilization to feel lost and bewildered, nor will we be the last, but this does not mean there is no remedy. Help has always been within our grasp: to ally our whole being with the building energies of the universe and to refuse to strengthen by default — certainly never by design — the destructive forces that are ever alert to attack the irresolute soul. Still, we must persevere, for once we make the choice, all the "devils" in the underworld of our nature will seemingly be let loose to test the integrity of our resolve. The more in earnest we are, the more subtle and persistent the resistance — not instigated by others, but by our own higher self.

There is nothing mysterious about this. Probably everyone has had the experience that when we determine to alter our habitual ways of thinking, everything and everybody appear to conspire against us. This is inevitable, for intensity of aspiration challenges the gods who are "jealous" of us humans who venture unprepared into their domain. Only those who have become near to godlike may enter. And since the gods are in a profound sense ourselves, the response to our importunate demands may be a release upon us of an avalanche of unexpended karma from past lives. This could be shattering to the personal self, but not to the part of us that *knows* deep within that we have longed to be tested to the limit of our endurance.

William Q. Judge uses the cryptic phrase "karmic stamina" in connection with aspirants who may find themselves momentarily in "a psychic whirl, or a vortex of occultism" into which others also may be drawn, and where the "germs for good or ill ripen with activity."* The outcome will depend not only on our constancy of will and selflessness of motive, but also upon our reserve of moral and spiritual endurance, our inbuilt stamina. The word stamina — from the Latin for "warp, thread, fiber" — is fitting here, for the warp of lengthwise threads on a loom is usually of stouter twist than the weft, as it is the foundation on which the cross threads are woven. The daily encounters and interactions with others and the impingements of events upon us are all karma: the warp represents the outflowing of past experience, while our reactions, being of our choosing, are the weft carried by the shuttle of the soul as we weave our present and future on the warp of the past.

All is not hardship and trial. Our inner god may be a stern taskmaster, but it is infinitely just and therefore infinitely compassionate. To be sure, potency of aspiration germinates whatever seeds of inharmony we have sown, but

---

**Letters That Have Helped Me* 1:20–1.

equally does it quicken the seeds of nobility in the character so that we are inwardly sustained and encouraged. In truth, it may shed a flood of light upon our path. Such a resolve finds resonance in our inmost self, and as we return life after life it leads us on and on, to take up the charge anew. Every day, every year, every lifetime, we infuse the ancient resolve with fresh vigor. Katherine Tingley speaks eloquently to this in her *Theosophy: The Path of the Mystic*:

> A vow is an action rising like a star high above the level of the common deeds of life. It is a witness that the outer man has at that moment realized its union with the inner, and the purpose of its existence, . . .
>
> At that moment the radiant path of light is seen with the eye of pure vision, the disciple is reborn, the old life is left behind, he enters a new way. For a moment he feels the touch of a guiding hand ever stretched out to him from the inner chamber. For a moment his ear catches the harmonies of the soul.
>
> All this and more is the experience of those who make this vow with their whole hearts, and as they constantly renew it, and constantly renew their endeavor, the harmonies come again and again, and the clear path is once more beheld.
>
> . . . Each effort carves the path of the next, and in no long time one single moment's silence will bring forth to the disciple's aid the strength of his soul. — pp. 53-4

Such a vow is a knocking at the door of our higher self. If the knock is genuine, the illumination and strength that pour into us can become a transforming influence that may help us to intuit the higher self's intent for our ordinary self. When the motive to serve humanity is fortified by will, our life is taken in hand by our higher self, and we find we are led into situations that test us to the core so that we may prove our worth and the depth of our aspiration — not for self-benefit, but that we may bring light and inspiration to others.

The higher self is our *real* teacher, our inner buddha. This is a time-honored truth: it places responsibility for growth, for inner advancement, squarely on ourself. We have no one but ourself to blame for our fumbles, no one on whom to shift our burdens. We are our own awakener, our own savior, for *we* are the steps we must travel and the truth we so long to find. Yet few of us feel adequate to fulfill the demands of our dharma, or self-disciplined enough to meet with equanimity the impact of daily karma. Trust is the key: to trust karma is to trust ourselves and to trust that we have the inner resources to handle whatever befalls. Having made the choice to live mindfully, there can be no turning back. We are not required, however, to take more than one step at a time; this is our protection, for by meeting life's challenges one day at a time we gather strength and sufficient wisdom for the daily need.

Once we grasp the fact that *we* are the path before us, never again will we know that aching loneliness of despair, for we shall have come in touch, if ever so fleetingly, with our light-source. Should periods of despondency return, they need not take firm hold, for a part of us, having entered into companionship with our higher self, remains en rapport with the larger fraternity of the spirit that touches every aspirant on the path. In proportion as we allow our buddha-nature to illumine our ordinary self will the

Tathāgata-light, the Christos-sun, irradiate our being and the path ahead. Since we are *one* humanity, the lighted path of a single individual makes the path of all others that much clearer.

It is a truism that no one can live always on the heights. We are obliged to return to the valleys of daily experience where we still have lessons to learn. But the panorama seen from the heights, short-lived as it may have been, is our rod and staff. It takes courage to allow our higher self to lead us into those circumstances that will bring to fruition old karmic causes whose effects on ourselves and on others must now be met. However, once handled, they will be done with. If at times everything seems at cross-purposes, and every effort we make is countered by opposition, this is to be expected.

The choice we made to pursue the compassionate way is by its very nature and goal an upstream endeavor. It is not a simple thing to go against the current; it demands courage to persist year in and year out along a course that, even if we know deep down is the true path for us, may at times appear quite the contrary to our personal self. Yet when we reflect on it, we are warmed and strengthened by an inner affirmation that we couldn't have asked for a more magnificent opportunity. To be allowed by karma to aid, in however minor a degree, in the compassionate order of the universe: this is to be given a boon that the soul over many lifetimes has silently yearned for.

We learn early that every aspiration must be sustained by self-discipline. Today people are stretching their souls, longing to rise above their ordinary little selves and glimpse a vision of what is beyond and within. Many of us, however, are so filled with our own ideas of what life is all about that we are like the student who came to the Zen monk seeking knowledge. "Teach me, Roshi, what Zen is." The Zen master invited him to tea. He started pouring tea into the teacup, and he poured and poured and poured until the student could stand it no longer and almost shouted: "But the cup is full. Can't you see?" The Roshi quietly said: "That is what your mind is like. You are so filled with your own ideas and opinions that there is no room for even one drop of wisdom. Empty yourself, empty your mind of all your preconceptions, empty your heart and your soul of all unbecoming thoughts and feelings, and you will be filled to abundance."

All of us know what is unworthy of ourselves. Striving to gentle the untamed propensities in our character is a type of purgation, a purification we can go through every day. This is what Paul meant when he said to the people of Corinth, "I die daily" — day after day he sought to be "reborn" interiorly. This is the "daily initiation," of which W. Q. Judge spoke — life itself, with its manifold joys and sorrows. Both have their temptations and trials, good fortune so called being often more difficult to handle than are the day-by-day frustrations and disappointments. The constant demand upon us to choose between the greater and the less, the selfless and the self-centered, brings us face to face with ourselves.

It is a matter of getting back to first principles: we start from within, from our central self. What *is* our motive? We tend to think of initiation as far removed from everyday happenings, but every time we conquer a weakness, every time we have the courage to see ourselves as we are, we undergo the testing by our higher self of our lesser self; we are proving the mettle of our character. "Fire tests gold, adversity proves strong souls" wrote Seneca, 1st-century AD Roman statesman and philosopher.* Any form of intense suffering, particularly when self-caused — through weakness of will, emotional instability, or being caught in a vortex of thought beneath our private inner standard — may become an initiatory experience. The word *initiation* means "beginning," the conscious turning of a new leaf in our Book of Life. To have penetrated the darkness of our individual hell and come up into the light of our radiant self, able to meet its demands, is a kind of initiation.

When we inwardly take a stand, we are forearmed for whatever comes; if we avoid doing so, when faced with really severe challenges we are unprepared to act responsibly. Using the wheel as a metaphor: by living in thought and aspiration as close as we can to the hub of our being, the turning wheel of karma will not crush us; but if we live on the rim or circumference of our lives, we are at risk of being ground down under the karmic wheel. This can and does happen more than is necessary; and it's a cruel thing to witness — and to experience. Nevertheless, we learn invaluable lessons in humility and compassion: not only do we gain immeasurably, but hopefully through it all we become sufficiently sensitized to help others see that if they ascend the radius of their being toward the hub of themselves, they

---

Moral Essays, "On Providence," 5, 9.

will find guidance, strength, and a light upon their path.

One of our noblest opportunities is to give confidence to our fellow humans that, no matter how fragile we may be or think we are, all of us have sufficient power to live our lives in an honorable, thoughtful, and self-disciplined way. We must allow our higher self to take charge of our life's destiny. Is there any greater gift one can offer than assuring another he has what it takes to handle his karma, with head high, regardless of how many times he may be knocked down? We are not alone in our struggles. Everyone has some cross to bear, some weakness of character to overcome; just so everyone has his or her strengths to build on. Simply put: if we have the fortitude to "hang in there" no matter how often we stumble or how far we fall, *there is no failure, only triumph*.

We are transcendent beings, cosmic in power, using human vehicles for growth and expansion of consciousness. Every man, woman, and child is here on earth as the result of aeons of experience, each of us entering life on earth as an ancient soul for a divine purpose. There isn't a single avenue of experience or duty that cannot be viewed through the eyes of our cosmic self. This puts a totally fresh perspective on our experience here on earth. Henceforth we know that, whatever our circumstances, we need never be downed by karma because the *long* perspective of many lives is a persuasive reminder of the unlimited resources on which we can draw.

Nature demands the utmost of her children to bring into flower their full potential. Every moment, day in and day out, we humans with our marvelous faculties of mind and intuition are contributing either to the well-being or ill-being of the human race, and by so doing leaving our impress on the noumenal or causal realms. Of course, no one should expect perfection from himself or another. Our goal is not to attain self-perfection; rather is it to emulate the life of service of those who come forth time and again as light-bringers, bearers anew of the ancient wisdom teachings. Whatever our role — laborer, housewife, professional — when we give the best of ourselves to fulfilling our particular dharma in order to advance the whole, our weaknesses take second place. We still have to handle them, but there is no call to focus undue attention on them.

We and the whole of humanity need to lift our consciousness from that which is disintegrative and dispersive to the level of the creative and constructive part of our nature. The most effective way to grow is to forget ourselves while getting on with our responsibilities. This seems rather ordinary, and yet it works because when we are absorbed in giving full attention to the task at hand, for that span of time we automatically put aside our worries. When we come back to them, often to our surprise we have a clearer view as to what approach to take.

In his *Yoga Sūtras*, Patañjali of ancient India urged control of mind and the myriad thoughts and images that willy-nilly pass through our consciousness: when we pour the fluid of our mind into a vessel, our mind takes that shape, indicating that we must be mindful where we focus our attention. A collateral thought is ascribed to another ancient Indian sage, Yāska: *yadyad rūpaṃ kāmayate devatā, tattad rūpaṃ devatā bhavati,* "Whatever body (or form) a divine being longs for, that very body (or form) the divine being becomes."* Inevitably, our consciousness will flow into the vessel of thought or emotion for which we have the greatest affinity. To modify and expand our present norms, we must modify and expand the existing vessels or break out of them. This takes courage and will. As we open ourselves to the light within, the light streams through us. As everyone in his or her own way is a light-bearer, so everyone who has the flame of brotherhood burning in his heart is bringing hope and courage into this world.

When we reach above the brain-mind to the heart of those with whom we have differences, a give-and-take of feeling and attitude by both parties occurs, and in no long time even the most intractable situation becomes possible to resolve. So it is in our ordinary dealings with our family or at work: when we spontaneously appeal to the greatness of the other person from the greatness in ourselves, we are naturally clairvoyant and recognize each other's inward need. There is beauty and magic in this, for we are aided by nature herself. As Katherine Tingley reminds us:

> Our strength lies in keeping positive; in holding a steady joy in our hearts; in a momentary meditation on all floating great ideas till we have seized them and made them ours; in a meditation with the imagination on the life of humanity in the future, and its grandeur; in dwelling on the conception of brotherhood.
> — *Theosophy: The Path of the Mystic,* p. 21

Those floating great ideas that continuously circulate in and

---

*G. de Purucker, *The Esoteric Tradition* 2:701.

through the thought consciousness of humanity are the source of our innate wisdom. We need simply to recover them, to recollect our inborn knowledge of them, and they will be our inspiration.

Every human being has full right to his own way of feeling and thinking, to his own idiosyncrasies. We need to respect each other's inner quality as much as we want ours to be respected. Assuredly, the most lasting contribution we can make toward bringing about a recognition of the dignity of every human being is to begin quietly within our own soul. Every person who really feels every other individual to be not only his brother, but his very self, is adding his quota of spiritual power to the moral force of the brotherhood ideal. We are *not* separate — *we are one life-wave, one human family.*

How and where do we begin? All of us have our home and professional responsibilities. These come first: we owe our family the fullness of our love, devotion, intelligence, and support. We take each day and trust that we shall read the karma of it with sufficient clarity to allow us to move forward as we should. Everything starts as a seed. Yet the miracle is that the tree is already patterned within the seed. Every phase of growth is matrixed in the seed-essence, in the invisible space (ākāśa) within the heart, that resides equally in the core of a star as in the nucleus of an atom.* We need to *live* to the full every moment and give each person and every smallest circumstance the wholeness of our heart and thought so that only the purest and truest quality of karma

---

*Cf. *Chāndogya Upanishad,* VIII, 1, 3.

will eventuate. Only then can we be responsive to the inner call of each individual or event. Even more than avoiding regrets or the feeling of having let another down by inattention or thoughtlessness, there would be only constructive, vitalizing energy flowing between us and those with whom we associate. Keeping in mind the reality of thoughts and their circulation in the astral light, were every one of us conscientiously to throw his heart into every moment of every day, holding fast to the ideal of service, the spiritual and mental consciousness of humanity would be touched with light.

We are part of a spiritual enterprise far vaster than our finite minds can grasp — associates in the outermost court, but associates nonetheless in a fraternity from whose central home stream the spiritualizing magnetisms that keep our planet and its humanities on course — insofar as world karma allows. It is infinitely inspiring to reflect that every aspirant is a participant in a continuing relay of strivers, each making it possible for the one coming after to have the hope and the energy to accomplish those achievements of the spirit that are awaiting the favorable time and circumstance to come to fruition. Passing on the torch of courage, perseverance, and devotion: each one alone of minuscule worth, yet together each a golden link in the buddhic chain of compassion and love whose innermost reaches are beyond sun and stars.

17

A New Continent of Thought

EVERYONE COUNTS. INTUITIVELY we know this, but do we grasp sufficiently the profound implications of this powerful truth? It is self-evident that thought and feeling move us to action, yet few of us are convinced that our private feelings and thoughts really do count in the totality of mankind. In this we err. It is no trifling matter that our merest emotion or thought affects to some degree not only our brothers of every kingdom, but also the universe. Truly, the magnetic interchange of responsibility and destiny among all living beings within the sun's domain is awesome: there is not a moment of our waking hours or during sleep (albeit in a different manner) when we do not exert some type of influence upon the auric atmosphere surrounding our globe in which the whole of humankind partakes.

How is this possible? In his first letter to A. O. Hume in 1880, KH wrote:

> every thought of man upon being evolved passes into the inner world and becomes an active entity by associating itself — coalescing, we might term it — with an elemental; that is to say with one of the semi-intelligent forces of the kingdoms. It survives as an active intelligence, a creature of the mind's begetting, for a longer or shorter period proportionate with the original intensity of the cerebral action

which generated it. Thus, a good thought is perpetuated as an active beneficent power; an evil one as a maleficent demon. And so man is continually peopling his current in space with a world of his own, crowded with the offsprings of his fancies, desires, impulses, and passions, a current which reacts upon any sensitive or and nervous organisation which comes in contact with it in proportion to its dynamic intensity.*

We are indeed "continually peopling our current in space" with the sum total of what we are. With every passing moment we are sending forth thought or desire impulses which, uniting themselves with elemental energies as and when they will, have capacity to nurture or retard the soul. By virtue of the continuous circulation of life-atoms, what we think and do affects not only ourselves and our family and environment, but likewise every living being on our globe.

Moreover, our thoughts and emotions are automatically registered on the astral light that surrounds our globe as well as on our own astral substance. Since the astral light is both receiver and expeller (as well as recorder) of the thoughts and emotions of every human being who has ever lived, at certain times when there is an opening it discharges both its lower and higher emanations upon the mass consciousness of humanity. This means that what we are now will be leaving its mark upon countless lives yet unborn, for the reason that every thought, emotion, and aspiration impressed on the earth's astral light in time reflects itself back upon ourselves and on others. What one *is*, therefore, is vastly important.

---

*Margaret Conger, *Combined Chronology*, p. 33.

The present thinning of demarcation between the astral and physical is proving of mixed value, and much depends on what we choose to identify with. At present, the astral light appears to be disgorging more than usual of its basest content; on the other hand, a greater number of persons are becoming responsive to energies from higher levels and, at times, receiving ideas and inspirations of sufficient worth to change many lives for the better. All the more reason to maintain a balanced outlook and not give way to feelings of hopelessness — either about ourselves or about the future of humanity. The debilitating influence such moods have on us infects the vital circulations of thought-energies through our planet. Too much is at stake for any of us wantonly to add negative thinking to the world karma.

Those subject to recurring depression are notably more sensitive than others to the cyclic highs and lows in nature and may oscillate rather violently between exaltation and despair. It is possible, indeed mandatory, to temper our reactions and focus attention on the golden midpoint between extremes. Every sage and rishi before and after Gautama Buddha knew and observed the ancient rule: when "unworthy images" fill the mind, instantly induce "worthy images." Then, with hatred, ill will, and selfish desire conquered, the "inner heart is made firm, tranquil, unified, and strong."* Katherine Tingley understood this well; she knew the power of visualization and urged her students, when gloom or despondency crept in, immediately to conjure up their opposites and thus initiate a new

---

*Majjhima Nikāya, quoted in *Fountain-Source of Occultism*, G. de Purucker, p. 35.

quality of energy. The influence of this new thought-current would in time prevail, and the student would feel a new sense of purpose, a new joy in his duties. In her book *The Gods Await*, she quotes a remarkable statement by her teacher:

> You know, the atoms of the human body become weighed down as a rule with the burdens of the mind — the irrelevant ideas, the preoccupations and anxieties. They go through series of changes momently, affected by the thoughts of the brain-mind. The lack of trust, the lack of inspiration that people suffer from — the hopelessness — bring these atoms down halfway to death. But they can be quickened to a kind of immortality by the fire of the divine life and attuned into universal harmony. — pp. 124–5

If at times it seems impossible to lift our consciousness out of the pit to the sunlight within, we can do the next best thing: give to the duty at hand the fullness of our attention. Before long the atoms that we had weighed down "half way to death" will have been transformed into the light-atoms of self-forgetfulness and generosity of feeling. We will have charged with light, and lightness, the full complement of our atoms, physical, mental, and spiritual. More importantly, such a private transmutation of attitude is global in its beneficent effect, radiating far beyond our limited circle of influence and giving hope and renewed stimulus to others.

The thought is enough to give binding assurance that every staunch effort to stand for the true does count and, when selflessly maintained, its potency for good is magnified beyond reckoning. I wonder if we realize how greatly we strengthen others by quiet, consistent response to the noblest within us; and, contrariwise, how potently we affect for ill those in the grip of fear or weakness when we indulge in unworthy thought or behavior.

Through the ages teachers and saviors have come among us and imparted the same challenging truth: that we cannot eradicate the selfishness and greed that are choking the soul of mankind unless we each root them out in our own character. Clearly this is not readily done, but just the fact that it may take an entire lifetime or many lives to achieve, is no reason not to begin. Among the Gnostic documents found in Nag Hammadi, one of the Sayings attributed to Jesus is relevant:

> . . . Whoever has
> ears let him hear. Within a man of light
> there is light
> and he lights the whole world (*kosmos*). When he
> does not shine, there is darkness.
> — *The Gospel according to Thomas*, 24

The determination to follow the mystic path of compassion opens a channel between the personal nature and the intuitive, higher self, and because of this the responsibility to oneself and all others is a hundredfold increased. Every time we indulge in petty or unkind feelings we close ourselves off from our inner light and thereby cast a shadow on the lives of others; conversely, every glint of radiance from the buddhi within helps by so much to illumine our surroundings.

When we see on television pictures of the terrible conditions that exist around the world, millions of ill and starving children for instance, it goes to the core of our being. Whoever of us is able to help relieve the distress and the hunger and pain should certainly do all that is possible — "Inaction in a deed of mercy becomes an action in a deadly sin."* But in our longing to feed the starving in faraway places, let us not forget our family at home or the needy in our neighborhood. Our responsibility is to fulfill our dharma, our inner duty where it lies.

Though we all long for the day when the desperate conditions of millions of our fellow humans will be relieved, we can be certain that when the dominant quality of a life is attuned to the heart cry of all others, this has a sustained beneficial effect on the group karma. Seeds sown in good soil germinate, take root and, in the course of time, flourish in season. So, too, thought and aspiration born of selfless yearning to ease the sorrow of man result in deeds, if not through ourselves, then through others karmically favored to bring to fruition what we had envisioned.

The work of healing and of compassion must be accomplished on the ideative plane first, if it is to have lasting effect on the physical plane. We must labor in the vineyard of minds and hearts and center our energies on rooting out the inner causes of the wretched conditions on our globe. While many of us may not be able to do much in a practical way to better the material conditions, there isn't one person who cannot contribute to the unselfishness in the world, who cannot strengthen the light forces.

When we are overburdened by the enormity of suffering

---

*The Voice of the Silence, "The Two Paths," p. 31.

endured by so many, we can circle the globe in consciousness and take note of the heroic labors of individuals and groups engaged in active philanthropic efforts to bring relief and restoration of hope. Not only is the exercise beneficial to our own state of mind but, more importantly, we lend force along inner lines to their altruistic endeavors. We cannot be grateful enough to those who, at great personal sacrifice and often at risk of their lives, undertake this saving work.

Light points are shining in different places, foci of compassionate helpers working in the world. They may not blazon forth their names or their accomplishments, but they are steadfastly at their post, which is more an inner than an outer post. We have spoken of the network of individuals that has existed ever since our self-conscious mind was quickened ages ago. This fraternity of illumined individuals labors in the quiet to stimulate the creative impulses in receptive human hearts. What we see is but the tip of an immense spiritual effort which has been in existence for many millions of years, and prior to that in previous world cycles. That network still exists, and the realization of a universal fraternity, hand in hand with the spiritual enlightenment of humanity, remain the "aspiration of the *true adept*" . . .

> And we will go on in that periodical work of ours; we will not allow ourselves to be baffled in our philanthropic attempts until that day when the foundations of a new continent of thought are so firmly built that no amount of opposition and ignorant malice . . . will be found to prevail.
> — *The Mahatma Letters to A. P. Sinnett*, pp. 17, 51

Today we are witnessing a revivification of the ancient dream of the onehood of all lives among a cross section of individuals committed to making it a fact in human relationships. There is indeed generated a power, a dynamic energy, wherever individuals of dedication are aspiring, even momentarily, in synchrony with the heart of Being. No one of us singly may be of particular significance, spiritually or otherwise; but collectively, each person contributing spontaneously of his unique quality of soul essence to uplifting mankind — who is to say what unpredictable and potent effect this might not have on inner lines? Jesus but repeated the ancient law: "where two or three are gathered together in my name, . . ." Spiritual teachings have power to elevate human beings; and whereas noble ideals in the thought-atmosphere have potency in themselves, when they are undergirded by individuals *living* those ideals, a certain magic can occur.

To think that our civilization is fated to continue its selfish and destructive habits is to prostitute precious thought power to negative ends. Conversely, to see ourselves as we truly are is to make a total change in our perspective: we are not separate, warring personalities but offspring of the cosmos, divine beings currently passing through the human phase for the sake of broadening and enriching our experience. While no one person can achieve single-handedly the miracle of world regeneration, millions of personal victories over self *can* have a miraculous effect.

Suppose that an increasing number of altruistically-minded people were to direct their aspirations toward high thinking and unselfish deeds, inevitably sufficient power would be generated to effect a spontaneous transmutation of humanity's life-patterns — from narrow egocentricity to largeness of compassion.

What the karma of the world will be is not ours to know; but if we simply and wholly offer our best, impersonally, we will be building bridges leading to that "new continent of thought" of which the Master speaks.

Sources

Aeschylus, *Aeschylus: Prometheus Bound* (1931), trans. Gilbert Murray, George Allen & Unwin, London, 1952.
Angus, S., *The Mystery Religions and Christianity*, Charles Scribners' Sons, New York, 1925.
Arnold, Edward Vernon, *Roman Stoicism* (1911), Arno Press, New York, 1971.
Barborka, Geoffrey A., *H. P. Blavatsky, Tibet and Tulku*, Theosophical Publishing House, Adyar, Madras, 1966.
Barker, A. Trevor, comp.:
　The Letters of H. P. Blavatsky to A. P. Sinnett (1925), Theosophical University Press (TUP), Pasadena, 1973.
　The Mahatma Letters to A. P. Sinnett (1923), TUP, 1992.
Blavatsky, H. P.:
　Collected Writings, vols. I, IX, and XII, ed. Boris de Zirkoff, Theosophical Publishing House, Wheaton, 1962–1980.
　H. P. Blavatsky to the American Conventions: 1888–1891, TUP, 1979.
　Isis Unveiled (1877), TUP, 1998.
　The Key to Theosophy (1889), TUP, 1995.
　The Original Programme of the Theosophical Society, Theosophical Publishing House, Adyar, Madras, 1931.
　The Secret Doctrine (1888), TUP, 1999.
　The Voice of the Silence (1889), TUP, 1992.
Cheney, Sheldon, *Men Who Have Walked with God*, Alfred A. Knopf, New York, 1946.
Conger, Margaret, *Combined Chronology: for use with the Mahatma and Blavatsky Letters to A. P. Sinnett*, TUP, 1973.

Cranston, Sylvia, *HPB: The Extraordinary Life and Influence of Helena Blavatsky, Founder of the Modern Theosophical Movement*, 3rd & rev. ed., Path Publishing House, Santa Barbara, 1993.
Darwin, Charles:
  The Descent of Man, D. Appleton and Company, New York, 1896.
  The Origin of Species, D. Appleton and Company, New York, 1896.
Doane, T. W., *Bible Myths and Their Parallels in Other Religions* (1882), University Books, New York, 1971.
Eckhart, Meister, *Meister Eckhart, A Modern Translation*, trans. Raymond Bernard Blakney, Harper & Row, New York, 1941.
Eldredge, Niles, and Ian Tattersall, *The Myths of Human Evolution*, Columbia University Press, New York, 1982.
Eliot, Sir Charles, *Japanese Buddhism* (1935), Routledge & Kegan Paul, London, 1959.
Encyclopaedia Britannica, Macropaedia, vol. 10, "Kepler, Johannes," William Benton, Chicago, 1974.
Frankl, Viktor E., *Man's Search for Meaning*, Beacon Press, Boston, 1959.
Green, Elmer and Alyce, "Mind Training, ESP, Hypnosis, and Voluntary Control of Internal States," Menninger Foundation, *Special APM Report of Parapsychology and Medicine*, 1973.
Guillaumont, A., H.-Ch. Puech, G. Quispel, W. Till, and Yassah 'Abd Al Masīḥ, trans., *The Gospel according to Thomas*, E. J. Brill, Leiden, 1959.
Harrison, Jane, *Prolegomena to the Study of Greek Religion* (1922), 3rd ed., Meridian Books, New York, 1957.
Harrison, Vernon, *H. P. Blavatsky and the SPR: An Examination of the Hodgson Report of 1885*, TUP, 1997.
Head, Joseph, and Sylvia Cranston, comps., *Reincarnation: The Phoenix Fire Mystery* (1977), TUP, 1994.

Hermes Trismegistus, *Hermetica: the Ancient Greek and Latin Writings which contain Religious or Philosophic Teachings ascribed to Hermes Trismegistus*, ed. and trans. Walter Scott, Oxford University Press, London, 1924.

Hitching, Francis, *The Neck of the Giraffe: Where Darwin Went Wrong*, Ticknor & Fields, New Haven and New York, 1982.

Hui-Neng, *The Sutra of Hui-Neng*, trans. Thomas Cleary, Shambhala, Boston & London, 1998.

Huxley, Aldous, *The Perennial Philosophy*, Harper & Brothers, New York and London, 1945.

Idel, Moshe, *Kabbalah: New Perspectives*, Yale University Press, New Haven and London, 1988.

I-tsing, *A Record of The Buddhist Religion as Practised in India and The Malay Archipelago (A.D. 671–695)*, trans. J. Takakusu, Oxford University Press, London, 1896.

Jinarājadāsa, C., *The Golden Book of The Theosophical Society: A Brief History of the Society's Growth from 1875–1925*, Theosophical Publishing House, Adyar, Madras, 1925.

Judge, William Q.:
Bhagavad-Gita combined with Essays on the Gita (1887–1896), TUP, 1978.
Letters That Have Helped Me (1891, 1905), 2 vols. in one, TUP, 1981.
The Ocean of Theosophy (1893), TUP, 1973.

Knoche, Grace F., *The Mystery Schools* (1940), TUP, 1999.

Kurtén, Björn, *Not From the Apes*, Vintage Books, Random House, New York, 1972.

Law, William, *The Spirit of Prayer: or, the Soul Rising out of the Vanity of Time, into the Riches of Eternity*, J. Richardson, London, 1758.

Marcus Aurelius, *Meditations*, trans. Maxwell Staniforth, Penguin Books, Baltimore, 1964.

Müller, F. Max, ed., The Sacred Books of the East, Oxford University Press, London:
Cullavagga, vol. xx, 1885.
Mahā-Parinibbāna-Sutta, vol. xi, 1881.
The Questions of King Milinda, vol. xxxv, 1890.
Saddharma-puṇḍarīka, vol. xxi, 1884.
Myer, Isaac, *Qabbalah* (1888), Samuel Weiser, New York, 1974.
Olcott, Henry S., *Old Diary Leaves* (1895), vol. i, Theosophical Publishing House, Adyar, 1974.
Pausanias, *Description of Greece*, trans. W. H. S. Jones, The Loeb Classical Library, vol. iv, Harvard University Press, Cambridge, 1979.
Plato, *The Dialogues of Plato*, trans. B. Jowett, Random House, New York, 1937.
Purucker, G. de:
The Esoteric Tradition (1935), TUP, 1973.
Fountain-Source of Occultism, TUP, 1974.
Man in Evolution (1941), TUP, 1977.
Radhakrishnan, S.:
The Bhagavadgītā, Harper & Row, New York, 1973.
The Principal Upaniṣads, Harper & Brothers, New York, 1953.
Ryan, Charles J., *H. P. Blavatsky and the Theosophical Movement* (1937), 2nd & rev. ed., TUP, 1975.
Scholem, Gershom G., *Major Trends in Jewish Mysticism*, rev. ed., Schocken Books, New York, 1946.
Seneca, *Moral Essays*, Harvard University Press, Cambridge, 1963.
Siémon, Jean-Louis, *Theosophia in Neo-Platonic and Christian Literature (2nd to 6th Century A.D.)*, Theosophical History Centre, London, 1988.
Skinner, Ralston, *Key to the Hebrew-Egyptian Mystery in the Source of Measures* (1875), Wizards Bookshelf, Minneapolis, 1975.

Sperling, Harry, Maurice Simon, and Dr. Paul P. Levertoff, trans., *The Zohar*, 5 vols., The Soncino Press, London and Bournemouth, 1949.

Stryk, Lucien, ed., *World of the Buddha: A Reader*, Doubleday, New York, 1969.

Taylor, Thomas, *The Mystical Hymns of Orpheus: Translated from the Greek, and demonstrated to be the Invocations which were used in the Eleusinian Mysteries*, new ed., Bertram Dobell, London, 1896.

Thomas, Edward J., *The Life of Buddha as Legend and History*, Kegan Paul, Trench, Trübner & Co., London, 1931.

Thompson, Francis, "The Mistress of Vision," *The Hound of Heaven and Other Poems*, International Pocket Library, Boston, 1936.

Tingley, Katherine:
  The Gods Await (1926), TUP, 1992.
  Theosophy: The Path of the Mystic (1922), TUP, 1995.

Titchenell, Elsa-Brita, *The Masks of Odin*, TUP, 1985.

Tsong-ka-pa, *Compassion in Tibetan Buddhism*, ed. and trans. Jeffrey Hopkins, Gabriel/Snow Lion, Valois, New York, 1980.

Verny, Thomas, M.D., with John Kelly, *The Secret Life of the Unborn Child*, Dell Publishing, New York, 1981.

Willoughby, Harold R., *Pagan Regeneration: A Study of Mystery Initiations in the Graeco-Roman World*, University of Chicago Press, Chicago, 1929.

Wilson, H. H., *The Vishnu Purāṇa: A System of Hindu Mythology and Tradition*, ed. FitzEdward Hall, Trübner & Co., London, 1864.

Index

Abortion 38-9
Adam and Eve, fall of 26, 87
'Ādām Qadmōn, four Adams 85
Adepts. *See* Brotherhood (of Adepts)
Ākāśa 114, 115-16, 181
Alchemists 4, 114
Allegory
  of Adam and Eve 87
  Jesus' crucifixion may be 97
  saviors' stories largely 89
Amṛita-yāna 131-2, 140
Ānanda, Buddha's death & 94-6
Anima Mundi 114-15
Apes and man 19-20, 21
Aquarian Age 123, 163-4
Armageddon 157-8
Asclepius, 159-60
Aspiration(s) 43, 166, 169, 175
  devachan and 46-7
  every, influences 71, 184, 190-1
  fostered by sons of mind, great teachers 24, 79
  intensity of, challenges gods 171, 172
  of pratyeka buddhas 130
  of true adept 189
  true meditation is 110-12
Astral
  body 34, 44, 119
  brain 55-6, 57
  chakras 107-9
  dangers of, plane 114, 119-20
  defined 114-16
  energies 116-17, 167
  entities channeled 118
  form of early mankind 20, 27
  line betw physical &, thinner 123, 184-5
  overemphasis on 155
  travel 118-19
Astral Light 127
  circulation of thoughts in 116, 182, 184-5
  defined 115-16
  influences from 108, 118
  regression and 56-7
Aśvattha tree, humans as 42
Ātman 35, 114
  as human principle 43, 118-19
  psychic centers and 108-9
  sūtrātman link to 165
Ātmānam ātmanā paśya 108
Atom(s) 8, 14
  are lives, conscious 13, 14, 29, 86, 101, 181
  body's, influenced by thoughts 186
  in human evolution 16, 46
  stamped with memory 37
  thought- 30
Avatāras, grace and 79-80
Awakening 139, 164
  global vii-viii, 70, 72, 107-8

HPB and current x-xi
of mind 23-4, 28, 87
three, sights of Gautama 132
'Ayin 84

Betrayal 41
by false teachers 152, 168
of Jesus 93-4, 96-7
Bhagavad-Gītā 5, 24, 72, 138
ātmānam ātmanā paśya in 108
first English trans. 102
rāja-yoga in 106 &n
Blavatsky, H. P. (HPB) 7-8, 70-1, 152
on astral light 115
current awakening and x-xi
held apes to be offshoots of man 19-20
life and work of 6-7, 145-8, 156
opposition to 148, 152-3
on original program of TS 153-5
pāramitās as given by 137-9
on psychic powers 121n, 122-4, 155
on sūtrātman 36
teachers and 148-52
on two paths 129-30
Bodhisattva(s)
Gautama or Siddhārtha 132, 134, 140-1, 144
path or ideal 135-6, 139, 142
Born in sin 87
Brain, memory in physical and astral 56
Brotherhood (of Adepts), Brothers, Fraternity vii

Blavatsky messenger of 148-9
publicity and 150
saṅgha or 144
spiritual effort of 151, 189, 190
we can be partners of 144, 182
Brotherhood, Human or Universal viii, 59, 165
in action 10-11, 105
lifeline to esoteric reality 105
pāramitās and 137, 139
transforming power of 157, 180-1
TS and 148, 150, 154, 156
Buddha(s) 43, 132, 143-4. *See also* Gautama Buddha
Ādi or Primal ix
of compassion and pratyeka 130-1, 142-3
future, Maitreya 162
Hui-neng on 141
inner 174
Buddhi 43, 187
Buddhist(s) vii, 89
Confession of Faith 143-4
on knowledge of past lives 61
Mahāyāna, pāramitās 137-40
metaphors ix, 10
two paths in, tradition 130-1
warnings about iddhis in, writings 120-1

Chakras, highest 108-9
Channeling 117-18
Character 56, 59, 67, 167, 187
building 62, 76, 80, 104-5, 127, 129, 142, 177
svabhāva or 36

Ch'i or prāṇa 106-7
Child, Children 32, 90
   of Earth and Starry Heaven 51, 53
   handicapped 39-40, 41, 66-7
   parents and 29, 37-9
   psychic leanings among 123
Chinese vii, 89, 91
   ch'i, yin, yang 106
"Chosen People" 6, 155
Christ. *See* Jesus
Christian(s) 3, 83-100
   early, knew Christ not unique 99
   mystical union of 4, 105
   second coming of 162
   Vicarious Atonement x, 76
Christianity 4, 83
   grace in 75-7
Civilization
   new type of viii
   regeneration of 190-1
Coats of Skin, Blindness 15-16, 87
Compassion 11, 150, 156, 170
   awakening of mind and 24
   chain of 89, 182
   civilization's renewal and 144, 190-1
   is behind all 39, 41, 47, 66-7
   justice and 63
   Passion of Christ and 81
   path of 104, 129-36, 137, 139-40, 175, 187
   saviors and 89, 93, 165
   work of, on ideative plane 188-9

Consciousness
   circle the globe in 189
   everywhere 13, 29-30, 34, 61, 101
   fetal, of first trimester 56
   initiation and 92
   lift our 107-8, 126, 179-82, 186-7
   missing link in evolution 20
   at sleep & death 42, 44-7, 110
Courage 65, 68, 111-12, 126, 175, 182
   to break vessels of thought 180
   pāramitā 139
Creationists 18, 21
Creed (Apostles') 98-9
Crucifixion and cry from cross 97-9
Cycle(s) 7, 34
   convergence of 123, 163-4
   initiatory 138, 164
   of a human life 16-17
   of life viii, 8
   lowest point of 16, 28, 161
   of necessity ix-x, 9
   planetary, of death and rebirth 158-61, 163

Darwin, Charles 5, 18-19, 20-1
Death 8, 33, 41-2, 44
   after-, processes 46-7, 54-5
   caused by soul 44
   early 48
   helping those faced with 64-5
   of Jesus, Buddha 93-8, 99-100
   near-, experiences 44-5
   second 46

Depression, Despondency 174-5, 185-6
Devachan 45-6, 47
Dharma 134, 143-4
 defined 71-2
 fulfilling our 179, 188
Dhyāna 106, 139
DNA, reincarnation, karma, and 37-8
Duty 178
 give full attention to 186, 188
 to search for truth 111

Earth vii, 42, 79
 child of, and Starry Heaven 51, 53
 creation of, in Qabbālāh 85-6
 destruction and regeneration of 33, 158-60, 162
 element 25, 29, 142
 evolution of 5-7, 14, 16, 27, 35
 past midpoint 16, 161
Eckhart, Meister, quoted 111
Ecology, Ecosystem 11, 113
Edda, on Ragnarök 159
Ego-centricity viii, 111
Elemental
 beings and psychism 119-20
 kingdoms 29, 30
 thoughts and, beings 71, 183-4
'Elohīm 26, 35, 85
Er, vision of 54-5
Evolutionary Arc 16-17, 161
Evolutionists 18-19
'Ēyn Sōf, 'Ēyn Sōf 'Ōr 84, 85

Failure(s) 49-50, 62, 93, 138

 there is no 96, 178
Fear 50, 114, 158, 187
 love and 126
Frankl, Viktor 63
Fundamentalists, perilous times and 158

Gautama Buddha ix, x, 3
 Ānanda and death of 94-6
 bodhisattva vow of 140-1
 enlightenment of 132-5
 on iddhis (siddhis) 121-2
 last words of 134 &n
 parallels of, with Jesus 88-9
 on unworthy and worthy images 185
Genesis 8, 18, 35
 Garden of Eden story of 26
 not intended literally 83
 Qabbalistic creation and 84-5
Gethsemane 93-4, 96-7
Gnostic(s) 3, 187
God(s) 50, 66
 aspiration challenges 171-2
 Christian 35, 75-7, 85-7, 98-100
 humans and ix, 13-14, 18, 85-6, 171
 inner 78, 92, 116, 172-3
 retreat of 29, 159
 -self, link to 165
 spark of 8-10, 59, 61
 turn to, without turning from self 167-8
 we are, will be 9, 13, 17, 26, 30, 60, 80, 86, 92, 139, 141
Gospels 81, 87, 89n

Grace and/or karma 75-81
Greatness in others, appeal to 180

Hades 51, 53, 92
Handicapped, karma and 39-40, 66-9
Harmony 60, 110, 116, 156, 158, 162, 165, 186
   justice and 63-4
Harrison, Vernon 153
Health 69, 103, 106-8
Heaven 97, 99
   child of Earth and Starry 51, 53
   creation of 85-6
   not predestined to 80
   passing away of 158-9
Henne, Viola, letter of 67-8
Heredity and reimbodiment 36-8
Hermes Trismegistus 159-60
Hierarchy of Compassionate Ones 132, 165
Hodgson Report critiqued 153
Hologram analogy ix
Hui-neng on buddhas 141
Human
   cycle of a, life 16-17
   future of, life-wave 17-18, 160-61, 163, 165
   transformation of, nature 135, 167, 186, 189
Humanitarian service vii-viii, 70, 189
Humanity 36
   adolescent 163
   astral light and 184-5
   early 20, 23-7, 85, 87
   guardians of 149-51, 156, 165-6, 189
   past midpoint of evolution 161
   people seek to transform vii-viii, x
   plight of 70, 80, 144
   we are one 11, 76, 142, 158, 175
Hymn(s) 51-2, 100
Hypnosis 55-7, 125

Iddhis 121-2
Ideas, Ideals 47, 71, 105, 151, 155
   bodhisattva 138, 141
   confusion of 50, 68
   Eastern 101-2
   floating great 180-1
   full of own 176
   power of 157, 190-1
   transforming 6, 33, 93, 102
Illness 66
   helping others thru 41, 64-5
   responding to grave or life-threatening 47-8
Initiation 52, 63, 138-9
   avatāras and 79
   daily 171, 176-7
   Jesus' life a story of 97-9

Jesus or Christ x, 3, 81
   betrayal of 93-4, 96-7
   death of 93, 97-8, 99-100
   dying for our sins x, 79-80, 88
   grace and 76-7, 81
   life of, interpreted 87-8, 90-2
   parallels with life of Buddha 88-9, 96
   quoted 36, 76-7, 86-7, 126, 187, 190

sun god of Christendom 100
Joy vii, 67, 73, 90, 96, 138, 140,
   180, 186
Judge, William Q. 9, 176
   founding of TS and 150
   "karmic stamina" of 172
   Western Occultism and 103
Justice 26, 47, 66
   karma and 63, 64, 76-7

Kalki Avatāra 160, 162
Kāma 43-4
Kāma-loka 46
Karma 35, 59, 125, 177, 181
   abortion, handicaps & 38-40,
     67-9
   avalanche of 172-3
   daily 139, 174
   grace and/or 75-81
   HPB's teacher on 70-1
   larger view of 39, 73, 178
   memory and 60-1
   national, racial, world, group
     30, 62-4, 70, 140-1, 144, 163,
     185, 188, 191
   nothing outside laws of 80
   old 66, 175
   we are our 37, 69, 72, 80
   -yoga 105-6
Keter, Kether 84
KH (Koot Hoomi) 149-50, 161,
   183, 189
Kingdoms of Nature
   links among ix-x, 18
   man passes through 15
   oneness of 30
   our thoughts affect 183

Krishna 106, 160-1
Kuṇḍalinī 107
Kurtén, Björn 19

Latin epitaphs 47
Law, William, on false spirits 167
Laya-center 37 &n
Lethe 51, 54
Life. *See also* Past Lives
   birth and death gateways of 44
   is, fair? 68-9
   sacred at all times 38
Life-atom(s)
   circulation of 30, 184
   defined 13n
   human evolution & 15-16, 37
   memory and 56-7
   Purucker on 13-14
   re-collected at birth 47, 62
Life-wave, future of human 17-18
Light 17, 28, 42, 71, 80, 88, 99,
   173
   -atoms, points 186, 189
   -bearers, -bringers 24, 179-80
   garments of 15-16
   inner 77, 110-11, 170, 177-8,
     180, 187
   Jesus on man of 187
Linga-śarīra 44
Lipika, karma and 62
Logos, Logoi 59
   cosmic 90
   seed- 34, 35-6, 59-60
   Word or 34, 83
Love x, 39-40, 64-5, 104, 182
   bonds linking those we 42
   grace and 75

practical 111
protective force of 126
Lyell, Charles 5

M (Morya) 149-50, 151
Macbeth 118
Magi and Jesus' birth 90-1
Mahābhārata 16, 24, 102
Mahatmas 149-53
Maitreya Buddha 162, 168
Man. *See also* Humanity
    Archetypal 85
    communion betw god & 50
    elements composing 43-4
    source of lower species 19-20
Manas 23, 28, 43, 124
Mānasaputras 24, 28-9
Māra 94-5, 133
Marcus Aurelius, quoted 48
Meditation 122, 139
    ways of, discussed 109-12
    Western occultism and 102-3
Mediumship 117-18
Memory 35, 37, 45
    karma and 60-1, 176
    Mnemosyne, goddess of 50-3
    of past lives 49, 54-6
    of physical & astral brain 56
    soul- 24, 29, 57, 136
Messiah, Messianism 90, 162-3, 168
Middle Way, Course 133, 135, 165
Mind 14, 117, 176, 183, 186
    control of 123, 125-6, 130, 138, 179-80, 185
    one of seven principles 43, 119
    quickening of 15-16, 23-9, 63,

87, 189
Missing Links 19-20
Mnemosyne, 50-3
Moirai 54
Monad(s) 43, 57
    evolution of 14-15, 17-18, 21, 34, 36
    one in essence 86
    spiritual, after death 46-7
Motive(s) 141, 173
    examine our inner 70-1, 76, 103-4, 158, 176
    for psychic development 119, 127, 155-6
    pure 32, 122, 126, 130, 167-8
Mystery(ies) 84, 115, 168
    Greek, stages of 104
    Orphic 50-3
    saviors' death &, -teachings 92-3, 98-100

Nārada 163
Near-death Experiences 44-5
Nemesis 60
Night, on retiring at 109-10
Nous 50, 52, 115, 119

Objective(s), TS 6-7, 154-6
Occult(ism) 123, 147
    is altruism lived 104
    vortex of 172
    Western 101-4
Odin, in windtorn tree 89-90
Olcott, Henry S. 146-7, 150, 154
Oneness, One 7, 102-3, 139, 157, 190. *See also* Brotherhood, Human or Universal

becomes many 3, 84-5
cosmic 59, 165
we are a 6, 9-11, 30
Opportunities 40, 69, 88, 175, 178
  seize or let slip 96-7, 127
  soul chooses 64, 68, 79
Oracles, ancient 50
Origen and reincarnation 32-3
Orphic hymns & mysteries 50-2

Panoramic Vision(s) 45-6, 47, 73
Pāramitās 122, 137-40, 169
Parent(s) 162-3
  effect of, on unborn child 37, 56
  of handicapped children 38-40, 66
  star 29, 46
Past Lives, remembering 49-50, 55-6, 61
Patañjali 102, 179
Path(s) 105-6
  of Compassion 104, 130, 132-36, 156, 187
  Eightfold 133
  our own 72, 111-12, 125, 173-5
  sunward 81, 99
  two 129-32, 139-40, 142
Paul 35, 43, 75-8
Pausanias 51-3
Pearl metaphor of oneness 10
Perfection not goal 168, 179
Piscean Age 123, 163
Planet(s) 46
  as animals 115
  to, after death 47, 54

death of 158
  as life-atoms 13-14, 17
  Wise Men and 91
Plants 15, 18, 30
Plato 3, 13, 57
  Prometheus story of 25-6
  vision of Er of 54-5
Poverty 69-70
Prāṇa 44, 106-7
Pratyeka 130-1, 139, 142
Prayer 110
Predestination 80
Prometheus 25-6
Prophets, false 166-8
Psyche 113, 139
  Nous and 50, 52, 115, 119
  our, invaded 108, 118
Psychic 123
  centers and ātman 109
  interest in 19th & 20th century 124-5
  invasion 125-6
  TS objective on, powers 155-6
  vanity 119, 122
Psychism 113-27
Purāṇa(s) 24, 160
Purification 54, 99, 104, 135, 149, 167, 176
Purucker, G. de 36-7, 68-9
  on apes and man 19-20
  on life-atoms 13-14
  on three wise men 91

Qabbālāh, Qabbalists 3, 4, 14, 43
  coats of skin, garments of light 15
  genesis in 83-5

Questions of King Milinda, The,
   on buddhas 130-1

Radioactive, all are 17
Rāmāyaṇa 102
Regeneration viii, 190-1
Regression, past life 55-7
Reincarnating Ego
   adverse conditions and 67-8
   after death 44, 46-8
   memory and 56
   monadic essence and 15
Reincarnation, Reimbodiment 31-4, 162
   abortion, handicaps, & 38-40
   heredity and 36-8
   regression and 55-7
Responsibility(ies), Responsible 15, 23, 80, 174
   daily, come first 120, 179, 181
   betw kingdoms ix, 18, 30, 183
   for our thoughts 63, 71, 142, 187

Sacrifice 26, 104, 189
   of Great Ones x, 129, 134-5, 144
   required 110, 112
Śambhala 151, 160, 162
Savior(s) 75-6, 81, 84
   cyclic appearance of 87, 169
   longing for 162-3
   many 3, 89, 90, 92-3, 100, 187
   we are our own 165, 174
Science, Scientific viii-ix, 6, 20, 145-6, 148, 154, 158
Second Coming 162

Secret Doctrine, The 36, 115, 145, 152-3
   awakening of mind in 27-8
   fundamental concepts of 7-8
Seed 35, 75, 104, 181, 188
   divine 8, 13, 26, 142
   -logos, -logoi 35-6, 59-60
Sefīrōt 85
Self viii, 30, 43, 60, 70, 72, 93, 114, 122, 125-6
   -becoming 35, 112
   -conscious 23, 26, 28-9, 87, 189
   -discipline 112, 167, 175-7
   higher 31, 39, 46, 59, 63, 80, 109-10, 118, 164-5, 170-1, 178, 187
   real teacher 112, 173-5
   -sacrificial karma 70-1
   see the, by means of the 108
   thread- 35, 61
   -transcendence 103-5, 107
Selfish(ness) 16, 26, 44, 64, 67, 71, 130, 156, 187, 190
Sensitives 120
Service 70, 109, 179, 182
   Meister Eckhart on 111
Shakespeare 80, 118
Siddhārtha 132, 140-1
Siddhi 121n
Sixth Sense 120
Skepticism, value of 168
Sleep 47, 53, 94, 100, 183
   death and 42, 45
Sol Invictus 100
Sons of Light, Darkness 28
Soul 8, 40, 46-7, 67, 71, 97, 105, 148

defined 119
immortality 6-7, 32-3, 38-9, 62
memory 24, 29, 50, 57
Stanzas of Dzyan 7, 27-8
Star(s) 35, 47, 83, 173
 alive 7, 13-14, 115
 of Bethlehem 90-2
 falling 14, 159
 linked with 8, 59, 182
 parent 29, 46
Sthūla-śarīra 44
Stoic(s) 59-60, 114
Suffering 32
 relief of 65-6, 143
 a stimulus 72, 177
 when overburdened by enormity of 188-9
Sun(s) 5, 35, 59, 88, 159
 Christ- 81, 97, 175
 evolution of viii, 8, 14
 gods 89-90, 93, 100
 Sons of the 92, 99
 we will become 17-18
Sūtrātman 35, 61, 165
Svabhāva 35-6
Sva-dharma 72

Teacher(s) 96, 149
 coming of great 79, 92, 135-6, 148, 162-3, 187
 of early humanity 24, 28-9
 higher self real 174
 HPB's 7, 70-1, 146, 150-1, 154
 Tingley's, on atoms 186
 would-be 166-8
Theosophical Society 145
 objectives of 154-6

 original program of 153-5
 origin of 147-50
Theosophy
 history of 3-5
 as modern movement 5-10, 151
 why name, chosen 147-8
Thought(s) 30, 46, 84, 93, 176-7, 186
 astral light and 56, 115-17, 182, 184-5
 atmosphere, -world 6, 17, 71, 79, 127, 157, 190
 Eastern & Western viii-ix, 6, 101-2
 elementals and 183-4
 new continent of 183, 189, 191
 reality of 182
 responsible for our 63, 71, 142-3, 179-80
 -transference 120
Tingley, Katherine 173, 180, 185-6
Tōrāh 84
Tree of Life, tenfold 85
Truth(s) 111, 133-4
 cyclic seeding of 3-5, 165
 half- 166-8
 impressed on early humans 24, 29, 166
 psychological, of Christian and Buddhist stories 83, 96
 within 50, 72, 114, 116
Tsong-kha-pa 131, 140

Vicarious Atonement x, 76
Virgin mother 88, 90
Visualization 21, 185-6

Vow 144
   Gautama's 89, 140-1
   power of 173-4

War 63, 160, 190
   physical & psychological 125-6
Wheel and hub metaphor 177
Will 28, 68, 78, 141, 172
   divine, or God's 66, 86
   to evolve 13, 23, 168, 180
   exercising, & inner growth 80, 110, 135, 139, 173-4
   intrusion on another's 125

   weakness of 117-18, 167, 177
Wise Men or Magi 90-1
Witches of Endor 118

Yāska 179-80
Yin and Yang 106
Yoga 102-3, 105-6, 108
   Sūtras 102, 179
Yuga(s) 160-2, 169

Zen story 176
Zohar 83-5